Through the Rose Window

Art, Myth and the Religious Imagination

Through the Rose Window

Art, Myth and the Religious Imagination

John F. Hayward

Introduced and edited by Kenneth A. Olliff

SKINNER HOUSE BOOKS

BOSTON

ISBN 1-55896-428-2

Printed in Canada

Cover design by Suzanne Morgan
Cover photo by Peggy Stevens
Text design by Sandra Rigney

Note: All Bible quotations are from the New Revised Standard Version unless otherwise specified.

Library of Congress Cataloging-in-Publication Data

Hayward, John F.
Through the rose window: art, myth, and the religious imagination / John F. Hayward; introduced and edited by Kenneth A. Olliff.
p. cm.
Contents: Art and the religious life—Imaginative truth and the Creator—The modest doorway of craft—Music and wild horses—Superstition, doubt, and faith—Living religion and a liberal tradition—Myth and the modern worlds—A new story of Creation—The Greek hero and the biblical anti-hero—Judaic mythology in modern Christianity—The incredible folklore of Easter—Hope and the Holy Spirit—Divine justice in the Hebrew Bible—Through the rose window—Prayers.
ISBN 1-55896-428-2 (alk. paper)
1. Liberalism (Religion) 2. Arts and religion. 3. Mythology. I. Title.

BX9869.H385 A5 2002
230'.046—dc21   2001057755

10 9 8 7 6 5 4 3 2 1
06 05 04 03 02

We gratefully acknowledge use of the following material:

Adaptation of "The Liberal Transmission of Tradition," from *Existentialism and Religious Liberalism* by John F. Hayward. Copyright © 1962 by John F. Hayward. Reprinted by permission of Beacon Press, Boston.

Homer, *The Illiad*, translated by Richard Lattimore, 1961, Book IX, line 406ff. Reprinted by permission of The University of Chicago Press.

Adaptation of "The Uses of Myth in an Age of Science" by John F. Hayward from *Zygon: Journal of Religion and Science*, volume 3, number 2 (June 1968), pages 205–219. Reprinted by permission of Blackwell Science.

Excerpt from *Gorgias* in *The Dialogues of Plato*, translated by Benjamin Jowett (fourth edition, 1953). Reprinted by permission of Oxford University Press.

IN MEMORY OF

Don Sternglanz, my college roommate,
who opened my mind

Muriel, his sister, my beloved wife,
who opened my heart.

Contents

Introduction

ART, ACCORDING TO JOHN F. HAYWARD, is any imaginative activity that allows us to transcend our experience and through our own efforts create something original, thereby sharing in the divine power of creation. Along with music, dance, and poetry, religion is an art form, a human endeavor that at its best and most profound moments allows us a glimpse into the heart of God. That insight is at the heart of this volume.

The title *Through the Rose Window* refers to a particular artistic creation, a stained-glass window mounted high above the altar of Chicago's neo-Gothic First Unitarian Church. This window is the inspiration for the final essay in this book and a model of Hayward's vision of religion and art. The rose window is a product of human skill and imagination. Our eyes receive its filtered images as angels, ancient imagery arising out of humanly invented stories. Yet the brilliance that shines through is not of our making; it is the light of God, characterized by mystery, wonder, and grace. Thus religion, along with other forms of art, mediates the divine to humanity. Through our imaginative capacity we appropriate the arts in such a way that they inform our spiritual lives.

Many of us in today's world feel a hunger to connect to something larger than ourselves, a yearning to drink from deep wells.

Individually and in communities of faith, we are questioning how we are to be in relationship with one another. We seek to know what is holy and how to approach it. We ask who we are as faithful people and who we are to become. This collection of essays is a resource for this calling. On these pages we are invited to witness one theologian's wrestling with God. Hayward turns to the ways in which the arts reveal the holy, underscores the wisdom of the biblical scriptures, and explores the vital role of myths in the religious life to address this hunger for religious inspiration and guidance.

Hayward expresses a deep appreciation for literature and the fine arts, especially those arising from Greek and Hebrew sources. His longtime mentor and colleague, James Luther Adams, nurtured in him a love of the arts and an appreciation for the prophetic biblical tradition. From studying Paul Tillich, Hayward learned to appreciate the power of symbols and myths in conveying the wisdom of the historical Christian tradition. Under Charles Hartshorne, Hayward studied Alfred North Whitehead's process philosophy, a twentieth-century naturalistic metaphysics that understands reality as dynamic and in continual evolution. This foundation was given theological expression under the guidance of Chicago School theologians Bernard Loomer and Bernard Meland. Hayward's theology thus integrates process thought's metaphysical framework with Christianity's concrete historicism, working out of and building upon this foundation in his own constructive direction in the areas of the arts and mythology.

Throughout his teaching career on the Federated Theological Faculty at the University of Chicago, Meadville Lombard Theological School, and Southern Illinois University at Carbondale, Hayward has kept one foot planted firmly in the church. Neither strictly an academic theologian nor a parish minister, Hayward has drawn upon the relative strengths of each as an aid and corrective for the shortcomings of the other. His sermons exemplify his theological rigor, while his scholarly writings reveal a passion for the pathos and promise of being human.

Like Hayward himself, the essays in this volume are at times winsome and poignant, at other times scholarly and profound. Some essays are emotive, strikingly personal reflections that seek to tease out the spiritual meaning of a particular event in his life. Others critique and construct theological concepts or give thoughtful interpretations of biblical texts and other works of art. Many of the essays work between these two poles, incorporating elements of each.

My connection with Hayward began while I was a seminarian at Meadville Lombard Theological School, affiliated with the University of Chicago. One of the kind things that my mentor, Professor J. Ronald Engel, did for me was to introduce me to his mentor, Professor John F. Hayward. While in seminary, I had begun to question the substance of my liberal faith. When I shared my struggle with Professor Engel, he guided me to Hayward's *Existentialism and Religious Liberalism* (Beacon Press, 1962). In that important work, I found a clear articulation of my own crisis of faith. Better than I could have done, Hayward had articulated my doubts about the liberal church and also my hopes, my deep investment in liberal religion and my fears about its inability to speak to my own life or to be relevant for the world of today. Not long afterward, Engel arranged a meeting with Dr. Hayward that was the beginning of a long and fruitful collaboration, which led to this volume.

In assembling the book, our goal was to represent the breadth of Hayward's theology in a format that would provide an accessible and practical resource for individuals and congregations seeking to deepen their theological reflection. Three major themes are pursued from a variety of angles and perspectives. The first theme explores the relationship between the arts and the religious life. Hayward develops a theory that religion is an invention of the human artistic imagination rather than a gift from a transcendent source. Through human skill and creativity, the arts express depths that are not readily available for rational analysis yet are deeply felt in human experience. The essence of religion is what lies behind art—the reality that the arts symbolically and poetically give voice to in fragmented and imperfect forms. A second theme of these essays is the religious function of myth. Hayward treats myth as a primary vehicle for religious expression in the liberal church. Myths are both literally false and symbolically true, or as Hayward puts it, they are "true fictions." The fictional aspect of myth recognizes the ultimate mystery of reality. The true aspect of myth recognizes the ways in which human consciousness interacts with something beyond itself to produce stories that can become revelatory. In the third theme, Hayward suggests a method of interpreting the Bible that allows us to appropriate the spiritual relevance of the biblical heritage without a coercion of belief or a sacrifice of the critical intellect. *Through the Rose Window* concludes with a collection of prayers through which Hayward gives living expression to his vision of religion and the arts.

Hayward's theology sustains a liberal view of religion that understands the primary sources of authority for the human religious quest to be experience, conscience, and reason, along with the rich spiritual resources that have been passed down to us. Part of what we in the contemporary liberal church might take from Hayward's work is a theological rationale for understanding religious liberalism as a *living* tradition. Hayward recognizes the centrality of both freedom of thought and inherited tradition in our religious lives. As a living tradition, liberal religion is the ongoing endeavor of faithful women and men to live in relationship to the accumulation of stories, ideas, feelings, images, and prayers expressed through the arts. Those who have come before us have shaped the way we see the world. They have influenced our language and our rituals, our ideals, and how we understand ourselves. This heritage is ambiguous of course, for in addition to the beautiful, the good, and the holy, our heritage is often barbaric. We frequently convince ourselves that the past has no claim on us, yet wholesale neglect of the past brings with it a vacuum of religious substance. As historical beings, located in specific communities and cultures and working out of our particular place in history, we are inextricably bound to our past even as we reject it. But the past is not fixed, and there is no one understanding of the liberal tradition that is decisive. Rather, the liberal tradition is dynamic and constantly undergoing revision. It speaks with many voices, many of which we are only now discovering, many of which we have neglected. We create and re-create this tradition at every moment. We who are the contemporary incarnation of liberal religion add our small contributions to this ongoing endeavor. We are the eyes and ears, hands, mind, and heart of a living tradition. We are not disconnected, isolated beings. We are part of something deep and abiding in which there is great wisdom, strength, and beauty. We are the stewards of the liberal faith; as this trust has been given to us, so we are responsible to pass it on to others.

My hope is that the reader will experience in these essays some of the joy I have known in working with Jack Hayward over these past years. His theology suggests resources for the sacred struggle that we in the liberal church are called to undertake. And yet reading his words offers us more—in addition to provisions for the journey, there is the pleasure of traveling in the company of a great mind.

Kenneth A. Olliff

Through the Rose Window

Art, Myth and the Religious Imagination

Art and the Religious Life

MARTIN LUTHER ONCE SAID that the fine art of music is "like a square dance in heaven." Perhaps Luther unintentionally reflected the ancient Greek belief that all human arts are gifts from divine Muses. The great reformer, who seldom did anything without passion, was passionately fond of music. And his enthusiasm bore fruit in his own and subsequent generations through the flowering of Lutheran hymnody and sacred cantata. This is especially the case in those greatest works of musical art, guided by prayer and Lutheran piety and explicitly dedicated to God—the works of Johann Sebastian Bach.

Few of the arts but music flourished in Protestant churches after the Reformation. The Lutheran condemnation of the abomination of images and idols and the thoroughly Puritan flavor of Calvinism on the continent and in England represented a prejudicial divorce between religion and the arts, a prejudice that is still in effect in most Protestant circles. Art has withered in the church and in the community generally because so few seem to be concerned to give it nurture. There is an exaggerated seriousness in the Protestant ethic—as well as in our busy world of science, technology, and business—where people feel they have something better to do than to dally in square dancing whether on earth or in heaven. "Work, for the night is coming" has been the law and the gospel to believers and unbelievers alike. And they are right so long as they and we allow ourselves to conceive of art as, at best, a pleasant dalliance or refreshing distraction from the main concerns of life. And because art has been classified not infrequently as play, it has been relegated to those sections of the population that have either the inclination or the money and leisure to devote themselves wholeheartedly to play, namely, children and the wealthy.

Granted that art is a kind of play, is it not also something more than play? Luther's "square dance in heaven" may suggest some celestial joining of play and work that is as serious and purposeful as it is delightful. It calls to mind the metaphor in the first chapter of Genesis wherein God undertakes the labor of creation for the joy of it and finds delight in the works of God's hand. The Greek satirist Lucian spoke, perhaps in jest, of the work of creation as play and of the sublime forms of play as somehow related to the highest levels of work.

Music has often been given a cosmic status, as in the phrase "the music of the spheres," as if the creation of the universe were a kind of joyful concert of separate powers moving into a universal harmony.

Music can be elegiac as well as celebrative. There is a kind of psychological linkage between the expression of misery in such a monumental work as Bach's St. Matthew Passion and that vast folk history of African Americans whose music gave birth to the blues. Surely there has been no more serious religious event recorded in the history of Christian faith than the New Testament story of Jesus' Last Supper with the disciples. Yet we are told that even as they sat under the shadow of death, they gathered not only to celebrate the Passover but also to sing together. Perhaps they could have done more than that. In the apocryphal Acts of John there is a remarkable story of how Jesus and all the disciples join in a dance after the Last Supper. I have no need to take this story as literal history. But I do find it to be an authentic model of a courageous action that might happen in any similar time and place. Here is John's story:

> He bade us therefore make as it were a ring, holding one an-
> other's hands, and himself standing in the midst, he said:
> Answer Amen unto me. He began, then, to sing an hymn and
> to say:
>
>> Glory be to thee, Father.
>> And we, going about in a ring, answered him: Amen.
>> Glory be to thee, Word: Glory be to thee Grace. Amen.
>> Glory be to thee, Spirit: Glory be to thee, Holy One:
>> Glory be to thy glory, Amen.

As the song mounts and the dancers turn and chant in an ecstasy of praise, they sing of what is happening to them, saying:

> Grace danceth. I would pipe: dance ye all. Amen....
> The Whole on high hath part in our dancing. Amen.
> Whoso danceth not, knoweth not what cometh to pass. Amen.
>
> —*The Apocryphal New Testament*, translated by M. R. James

This story describes these men as making a joyful noise unto the Lord not for the mere pleasure of singing, nor to distract themselves from their anxieties. A single song and dance will never make them forget the doom that hangs over them. This is ultimately serious music, ultimately serious dancing. It is their way of laying hold of the only power left to sustain them in their looming tragedy to the end. They are not sustained for long. Note that in the gospel stories of the crucifixion, the disciples are demoralized and scattered by the murder of Jesus and that Peter publicly denies having any association with him. But in this last Passover, Jesus and his followers do not fail to connect themselves to a sacred history larger than their own personal lives. They give form and expression to a power that transcends them and, if only for a moment, acknowledge that power on the threshold of death.

This is the religious dimension of art—that mortal human beings give form to the formless, that certain events flowing through them as human experience come forth out of them as music. We do not choose at what point on this planet and in what era of time we are flung into life. We had no part in making the stuff of our own bodies or the elements of our initial dwelling places. If we have any freedom of choice, it lies in the area of giving finer form and grace to the life and environment in which we actually find ourselves. If we are free to make or hear music out of what is miserable as well as what is favorable, if we can sing or respond to song in our deserts as well as in our gardens, we have some hope of amazing grace. We pay this kind of attention to artistry not primarily for the sake of aesthetic delight but for the sake of keeping alive the kinship of humanity and our own personal humaneness.

This means that art can have an important place in every human life and is more than the province of a gifted few. No house should be built with any seriousness without some degree of art; no important letter should be written without an inescapable thrust toward artistry; no family or church celebrates good fortune or gathers itself against the onslaught of trouble without some degree of artistic arrangement of the activities of its members. For in all these things, art is the creation of new forms (or the release of old forms) whereby fallible people reach a new level of individual meaningfulness and mutual support. In its barest essentials, art is no more than the effort to make human life more livable and lovable.

To be sure, as in all things, there are those favored few whose talent is at the level of fine art. But this sort of genius would be utterly speechless and powerless if there were not lesser levels of art widespread throughout human life to produce and receive the higher levels. The great artists speak to the largely inarticulate artist in each of us. Otherwise their voices are solitary and unfruitful. Without the human passion for art expressed in every level of home, family, church, vocation, and community, our world would lapse into chaos. And even when chaos is present, the redemption of its victims often begins with their God-given energy and desire to transform misery into music. A song of sadness, defiance, even despair, by virtue of its being a song and not merely an unformed expression, is the beginning of redemption.

There are several practical conclusions to be drawn from these general ideas concerning the place of the arts in the religious life. The most obvious is the importance of educating our children and ourselves in the appreciation of the human artistic urge and performance. This means placing art and art education far higher on the list of human learning than it normally occupies. Many of our schools spend thousands of dollars on athletics and pennies on the arts. And this is so mainly because most of our families encourage their children to become involved in sports rather than in craft and the appreciation of craftsmanship. I believe athletics to be a splendid form of craft and art, but not sufficient for civilization in and of itself. Children love to make music, pictures, models, plays; they enjoy the reading and recitation of poetry. The best musicians reach their musical powers mainly because they began at a very young age. Language itself is an extremely complex art learned very early in life. The more children are read to and spoken to colorfully and expressively, not simply with orders as to what they must do, the more they will develop that mixture of critical thinking and imaginative innovation that all good speech requires.

The most artistic center of family life is the dining table. Children, parents, and friends need to experience the communal delights of gastronomic art as well as the kinds of fun and conversation that grace these delights. Such learning is impossible if there is no table, no gathering, just a series of snatched meals consumed standing up and ending abruptly with the rush for other activities. How can the formalities of a church service hold the attention of persons who neither care nor know how to serve food courteously and graciously?

Friendship is itself an art: how to be generous, how to express thanks for generosity received, how to withhold unnecessary criticism, how to praise what is praiseworthy, how to forgive someone without belittling them, how to accept forgiveness without shame. Friendship may be spontaneous and delightful for awhile, but it must be cultivated to be lasting.

The art of communal action is obvious in sports, but not so obvious in the communities of education, business, and government. How can large groups of people working together learn to bridge the sometimes conflicting values of individual initiative and communal cooperation? Of late we have become much interested in conflict resolution, a necessary art. But that art would be needed less in a culture such as America's—where the value of individualism is paramount and competition is highly honored—if our means for engendering and maintaining community were given greater importance.

In worshipping communities the great moments of love, birth, and death should find their proper symbolic expression in artistic words and music. The couple being joined in marriage deserve to celebrate their love before God and in the presence of a beloved community. The child being launched into life and society needs to be joyfully affirmed and guarded by the love of its future congregation. Weddings and christenings are joyful occasions easily open to artistic celebration. However, in line with the legend of the singing and dancing on the eve of Jesus' death, funerals and memorial services also require some kind of hallelujah. No memorial tribute is complete without a blend of happy memories of the dead with recollections of his or her human fallibilities. Human life is all the more lovable when it is measured against the ambiguities of its powers.

It is during all the sacramental events of religious life, whether in general or special services, that the artistry of the religious community serves to bring the sacred core of life into visible and audible reality. Many years ago theologian Paul Tillich and Alfred Barr, founding director of the Museum of Modern Art in New York, founded the Society for the Arts, Religion, and

Contemporary Culture. That organization exists and flourishes to this day. In its statement of purpose are these arresting words:

> Religion in isolation from the arts is starved of concrete embodiment of its insights into the fullness of human life. Art gives religion the eyes to see ourselves in all our dimensions, the ears to hear the voice of our inner lives and the instruments with which to communicate with each other. At the same time, the past suggests that the arts realize their potential most fully within that transcendent, unifying vision which is the heart of religion.

Seeing ourselves in all dimensions emphasizes the importance of confession as well as celebration. A religious community is not a commonwealth of perfection, a congregation of genius. We are all small vessels of life, rather shabby at times, at times broken. It is our human dignity—and also the glory of God—that from such a variety of broken vessels there can arise a marvelous and ever-changing harmony, an unending procession of song and artifact, word and ritual, thought and gesture. Ancient people delighted themselves with the thought that the stars of heaven made music. People today can listen on pleasant spring evenings to the singing of frogs in their muddy swamps or the cry of lone birds in their deserts. Each person dwells midway between earth and sky. Their music is earth-bound and heavenly. They carry within themselves the mystery of creation. And in giving voice to the mystery, they may tell themselves and others that all the music of earth and sky are one, that the voices of frogs, birds, stars, and human beings belong to one chorus whose spirit and creator transcends and includes them all.

All "home arts" seek a wider communal focus in the life of one's religious community. Here I believe the old Protestant rejection of craft and art needs to be reversed. The church, the synagogue, and the mosque need to be beautiful in order to be effective. Sacred space is not formed wholly by the good will of its tenants. It must be designed for beauty as well as use, furnished with the means for excellent music, and adorned with visual and literary reminders of its unique traditions and history. Its primary voice is twofold: Hallelujah and Miserere. People crave to be led into an ecstasy of celebration for the very gifts of life and sustained in their mourning for all losses, guilts, and inadequacies. Love and joy, suffering and death are the principal subjects of fine art. These same elements of life must be present, highlighted, and dramatized in our acts of worship. The means for these endeavors should be drawn both from ancient tradition and from the contemporary scene.

When history and antiquity meet and find fruitful and mutual reflection with the present day, the miracle of religious enlightenment occurs. The church and synagogue seek the art of joining the witness of the ancestors with the experience of ourselves, their descendants. Not that we are slaves to their authority, but rather brothers and sisters with them in the endless ambiguities of human good and evil, joy and sorrow, love and death. And even as an artist is both inspired by and dissatisfied with the arts of the past and must invent some novelty beyond their example, the same is true of the religious mission. We listen to the past; we invent new expressions and applications of its perennial themes.

Imaginative Truth and the Creator

MY LONG ASSOCIATION with the arts has taught me to respect the human imagination and to see in its seeming make-believe the astonishing lineaments of a solid truth not otherwise available. Imaginative truth is truth, not in the sense that it is verifiable but in the sense that it brings to consciousness things we seem to have known all along. When we say something via the imagination, we may remind ourselves of what we have felt but never thought of before in just that way. Imaginative truth is as real as the numbers of fingers on one's hand. But it is a truth less transferable and less negotiable than the truths of simple quantities.

Because of the vagueness that haunts even the clearest imaginative truth, the works of imagination—that is, the work of the communication of images—must begin at some point of familiar human experience. I begin at such a point by asking you to contemplate the human hand, not the bare abstract statistic of its five digits, but the complex character and qualities it displays.

Was there ever an instrument more designed for opposite, even contradictory tasks? Make the hand into a fist and you have a cudgel, a weapon of war. Open it wide and vary its shapes and you have a teacher, either the simple teaching of the traffic cop who tells you when to stop and go or the complex teaching of the symphony conductor who elicits from the elusive shapes of music perennial forms of universal human feeling. The hand clenched in anger is the same swift and tender instrument that soothes, comforts, and cherishes. The hand, above all, is an explorer. A surgeon puts her fingers into the very sanctuary of the human heart and rearranges its plumbing without being able to see every detail of her work. She must finally trust the wisdom of her fingertips to save a life. Without her mind and its far-reaching plans, her fingers would be helpless. But after the mind has proposed the event, the fingers must finally dispose it. And in their skill the issue is decided.

As the surgeon, so the artist. The mind, that storehouse of dreams and central dispatching point of all human projects, sends its constant messages to the artist's hands. But the hands themselves discover what can and cannot be done; the fingertips finally answer the mind's question as to whether the dream can be equaled or even surpassed. The hand can discover qualities the mind had not dared to dream. And the delighted mind then marvels and rejoices at what the hands, in their intimacy with material, were able to reveal. The artist's hands dance to the bidding of the mind, sometimes in spite of the mind's censure, and when manual skill and dream are fulfilled, the mind rejoices after the fact.

This is true even in writing. The best way to know what one thinks is to speak or write via the dance of tongue or hand. One's mind does not appreciate the full extent of the flow and meaning of words until the hand and pen have duly set them forth on paper. Robert Frost wrote, "A poem begins in delight and ends in wisdom." The play of words, if successful, brings truth to life.

Let us generalize and say that there are three stages to the artistic impulse. The first stage is mental: The mind has an idea, a plan, or perhaps just a vague urge more like a dream. The second stage is material: The hand or other parts of the body go to work testing whether any dream or plan so conceived and so proposed can in fact exist and endure. The third stage is again mental: In face of the fashioned material, there is a new meaning to be edited, enjoyed, and woven into life. All creating, whether casual or concentrated, pragmatic or artistic, participates in this threefold pattern of dreaming, doing, and contemplating. Not until the contemplative activity is any creating complete.

All nature seems to participate in this threefold rhythm. The winter tree, with next year's dormant buds and sap unrisen, is like a long sleeper dreaming of the spring. With the warm weather's coming, the sap rises and the leaves begin their varied and seemingly aimless experiments in sprouting. Each leaf does its own sprouting and growing, probing its own space like the probing fingers of the surgeon or artist. The leaf responds to the tree's law, but its way of growing and its chance meetings with sun and shade and wind and storm finally are its own. The tree arrives at its new state only after spring's million experimental leaves have done their work. A new total effect, related to but different from last year's growth, is there to be used and enjoyed by the bodies of birds, squirrels, and small children and by the eyes of everyone.

Let us stretch our imagination further and move out from the center of human activity. Let us suppose the whole universe to be endowed with the quality of artistic experiment. Conceive of the universe as a vast organism with myriad fingertips probing and exploring, testing what can be done. And suppose that in spite of the multiplicity of these experiments, in spite of their occasional hostility, frequent collapse, and failure because they work at cross purposes, this universe is nevertheless one reality. That is to say, no experiment is wholly self-subsistent or wholly cut off from the foundation of power and energy and pattern on which it rests. This universe would imply a vast artistic impulse moving through all parts of the whole, sending its power and its dreams out to the fingertips. These fingertips are small, fragile, transitory realities—casual winds, wandering stars, flowers, animals, rivers and streamlets, and you and I. Driven by an impulse coming from depths beyond depths, from a past beyond all histories, we move through life, groping and learning, trying and failing, and trying again—and every now and then achieving something eminently good and wonderful. We are not only fruitful, multiplying after our kind but we are also given stewardship over the earth to care for and replenish it. We fashion its materials. We conserve its resources, strengthen its gardens, trees, soil, wildlife, even its waters and air. We have children of our flesh and children of our hands.

No one could create without the primal impulse of deep wisdom, which we did not create and which comes through us from earliest times. But given this impulse, it is everyone's free and unique task to do with it what one alone can do, what no general impulse could achieve until it were specialized in a distinct individual. Just as each fingerprint is unique among all the billions of otherwise similar human fingers, so each fingertip of the universe is unique among all the regularities of form and substance that have pushed us into being. We live in response to a huge behest, but what we do is ours alone to do.

If we fail to act, it is a loss to the whole. Or if we are cut off from acting by premature death, it is a discernible, if minute, loss to the whole. When parents lose a child to death, they cannot be comforted by the thought that the loss of one child makes no difference in this populous world. This child is their child; they know its uniqueness; they know that the child is literally irreplaceable. Perhaps you can imagine the vast love of God, which would regard every concrete event as unique and precious, noticing the least sparrow as it falls to earth.

If God were such, it would follow that all deaths would be sorrowful, even the deaths of those obstreperous creatures we call our enemies. We might cherish the glory and majesty of some high human achievement like the Golden Gate Bridge in San Francisco. But we should love also the small bronze plaque recording the names of those who died in its construction and never lived to see that great wonder complete and whole.

If God were such, what a huge arena of endless experiment would be present for observation! Since I know of no other populated planet but this one, I can only imagine the divine watchfulness of the fate of the earth. Wind and weather are among the experimenters, the pioneers of the planet. At the south end of Lake Michigan or all along the shores of Cape Cod, these tireless agents—seeming as aimless and careless as children in a summer meadow—cross and recross the land and waters. Air blows, waves pound, a grand noise—and the sand dunes are shaped and sculptured afresh every day. What would be God's constant delight and astonishment at all sands, all the Saharas in all the galaxies of space? God would be filled with unimaginable cosmic delight, hearing the roarings of the seas, the hallelujah choruses throughout space: "Let the heavens be glad, and let the earth rejoice; let the sea roar, and all that fills it" (Psalm 96:11).

If God were such, all this vast activity could be the fulfillment of the divine creative impulse. It would be as a song of praise, not because God is weak and needs encouragement, not because God is a tyrant and needs flattery, but because God takes delight as these agents recreate and co-create a universe. And God would love the fullness of it and rejoice with them. For as "The heavens are telling the glory of God; and the firmament proclaims his handiwork" (Psalm 19:1), so God exults in the glory of the heavens and the firmament, which bring the work of divine power into being. As in the last day of the original creation, so today God looks abroad and sees everything that he has made, "and indeed, it was very good" (Genesis 1:31).

As with the heavens and the firmament, so also with humanity. We are not so vast as the firmament, but our intricate making, our delicate artistry has its own unique goodness and perennial delight. In our poetry, dance, and music, we roar like the sea or speak as gently as the whispers of spruce boughs and bird wings.

Our creating is endless, transmitting to all the gross materials of earth the fine finish of human intelligence. Brother and sister to the fish, we swim deeper and faster; akin to the birds, we fly higher and farther. Our history is the most astonishing of all the many-colored dramas of our world. The tapestry of our deeds is too great for one human mind to encompass or remember.

If God were such, it follows that God would look upon humanity and rejoice. It would also follow that God would be fearfully dismayed by these human children and co-creators. For in observing humanity the divine vision would find in us—more than in all winds and waters of the world—pride, anxiety, haste, frustration, rage, malice, and destruction. The human world, filled with hot impulse and fear, striking out in blindness or savage cunning, could come close to ruining the lovely theater of our experiments, could lay waste the green and blue and gold world wherein God had lovingly established us. As creator of the grand design, God would have to interfere, to chasten, destroy, and root out human evil, a grievous discovery. It is better to bless than to punish, to rejoice than to restrain. It would mean less than nothing to God if we were to commit these horrors in the belief that such deeds were a divine offering or the fulfillment of a divine will. As Hebrew Scriptures implore:

> Will the Lord be pleased with thousands of rams,
>   with ten thousand rivers of oil?
> Shall I give my firstborn for my transgression,
>   the fruit of my body for the sin of my soul?
> He has told you, O mortal, what is good.
>
> —Micah 6:7-8

First, "to do justice," nobly and boldly and wonderfully, fashioning the state and the houses of the state and its laws and deeds of voice and hand and all the ingenuities of love and cherishing into ever more beautiful forms. And second, "to love kindness," even as God does. For the world is teeming with experimenters like you. And if you must fail, so might many of them. If you must cause pain, so might others. If you are to be free to continue the Grand Experiment with its risks of failure and pain, so must they be free. Better to have mercy and know love and all its imperfections than to bear the empty silence of conquest and death. And third, "to walk humbly with your God," for it is by divine might that yours is established, by divine dreams that yours are possible, and by divine joy that your own reaching after joy and achievement are made full.

If God were such, it would follow that God would carry a great burden of sorrow, surpassed only by indelible might and joy. Periodically, many skillful fingertips would be mutilated, many choicest champions destroyed in wars, in prisons, in law courts, in cruel folkways and in sophisticated falsehoods, in endless misbegotten enterprises—all seeming to concentrate in a vast wooden cross. Yet God's sorrow would be the fuel to the divine strength, causing it to shine all the more brightly in every darkened hour. God would not let us sink into the wretchedness we had so skillfully designed for ourselves, but always goaded by divine restlessness, we are moved to seek for the divine design. If we crucify our kind, God would send such a light upon that dread event that some would become utterly blind; others, opening their eyes, would see the divine love and be bold to love again, casting abroad once more the radiance of their own love.

Thus, God in this form would pursue us, dissolving our wickedness in tears, engendering our righteousness in the courage of desperation. God would not let us go until love and hate were given their right names and the merest child could see and understand.

And finally God would remember those who suffered for righteousness' sake. Though they were dead, the very quality of being that was uniquely theirs would be added to the divine treasury of creative impulse for all future times. Because they were, the world would be permanently affected.

I have put all these thoughts conditionally, appealing to your imagination and reason as to how it would be if in our time one might spell out some of the attributes that might belong to the Creator. Like you I live in darkness and what I say here is not a kind of "knowledge" I can demonstrate and verify. It is not meant to coerce your judgment but only to tease it into a new freedom. It is meant to show you that modern life and experience, art and poetry, and our biblical heritage can all combine to produce an image of what humanity might honorably love and serve all our days. I can show you many images, yet I cannot create any image native to you. If I thought I could, I would be disobeying my own rubric; namely, that each of you is a probing, experimenting finger of the universe. The shape, quality, and character of your faith may be externally suggested on every side by many people in contrary ways. What is, has been, and will be your faith lies largely in your own history, finally in your own hands and mind.

The Modest Doorway of Craft

ART, ESPECIALLY THE FINE ARTS, is an exalted subject normally connoting the holdings of special museums and wealthy patrons, and when studied as history at the university level, there is usually a search for levels of genius. But the arts are also crucial threads in a wider tapestry of culture, where they can be recognized as pleasurable and meaningful parts of everyday life and occasionally sublime. I ask you to ignore, at least for a while, those pictures of a frowning Beethoven storming through the clouds of heaven or the magnificent scowl of Michelangelo's David, who seems to be casually risking his life not only against Goliath, but also against the larger menaces of Fate itself. Do not associate art too closely with Homer's grandeur, Milton's epic scope, or the sublimity of *The Divine Comedy*. It is best to approach these literary monuments as bravely and unafraid as they approach you, even with a little healthy disrespect and humor, as Dorothy Sayers did in her *Introductory Papers on Dante* when she began an essay entitled "The Comedy of the Comedy" with these words: "I have sometimes played with the idea of writing a story and dropping into it, casually and without comment, the following sentence: 'George was curled up comfortably in a big arm-chair, chuckling over *The Divine Comedy*.'"

Let us then enter the lofty theater of the arts through the modest doorway on the lintel of which is inscribed the word *craft*. Let us not speak of the arts and crafts as though they were separate and unequal, as though *the arts* had a mighty voice and flair, while *craft* suggests the soft speech and modesty of the workshop and the gift shop. Let us reverse the order and say "craft and the arts" and think of craft as the mother of the arts and the arts as her children. Craft is the irreducible origin and beginning of all art. Some works of craft, partly because of their substance and the caprice of human taste and marketing, move into the realm of fine art and sometimes out.

With children the learning of the first and simplest crafts of voice, hand, and body is entirely indistinguishable from the pleasures of play. Three of the great crafts leading to art in the adult world continue to recognize in their self-description this unity of work and play: One plays a role in a play, plays the piano, or plays shortstop in a ballgame. Too bad that only theater, music, and sports have kept the word *play* in their essential vocabulary. Although artists have dry periods and temptations to despair, beyond all negatives they must, like children, continue playing, whether with paints or T-square and triangle, wood or stone, or the rhythmic movement of their own bodies.

Craft grows out of random play, and the joy of playing grows from an increase of craft. Of the increase in human craftsmanship there is no end, no perfection, only an ever-changing capability driven by the instinct to play, to play well, to play better. A mathematician playing with formulas, a violinist playing with her instrument, an actor with his role, a sculptor with hammer and chisel, dare not be merely repetitious in the way they work their skills. They must also play them, uniting the orderliness of learned work habits with the risk of unhappy mistakes of play, using certain known tools of routine to reach unforeseen levels of achievement and delight.

When my friend Cathy Pantsios, a skilled chef, plays with her stove, she must humbly respect what it can do that she cannot. As she says, she does not cook, the stove does. She must respect its powers and limits, even as she seeks to invent new culinary delights. She crystallizes the essence of her craftsmanship in this lovely sentence: "At the end of the night when I break down and scour the stove, it is with a tenderness and humility that I hope I can somehow express to this not-so-inanimate object the respect I feel for it."

Her key words are *tenderness, humility,* and *respect.* The wood carver must respect the grain of wood and the restraints put on her by the relation between grain and knife. A stonecutter or sculptor has to be patiently respectful of the intricate grain in different kinds of rock. How delicate are the measurements of a good violin or the weight of its bow! All materials, whether to be externally shaped or internally used, are full of natural felicities and natural perversities that the craftsman ignores at his peril. Luciano Pavarotti speaks of his voice as his "instrument," which he must care for, exercise, and rest exactly as he might respect a Stradivarius violin. How far can a dancer push and strain her own body before her craft literally fails?

I do not mean to imply by these considerations that an artist's primary job is to copy or be a slave to nature. All art is the invention of the artist, as well as a reflection of nature's own fertile artistry. The most primitive crafts and arts used to be and often still are devoted to making the invisible gods visible, not simply to replicating the visible forms of nature. The primitive craftsman was an inventor playing with social intuitions of divine archetypes, not only a designer of forms for human use or delight. The same instinct permeated early Christian art right down to the dawn of the Renaissance. Scenes, figures, colors, and shapes were "inaccurate" depictions of the noonday images of the eye, but they were faithful to the spiritual images of the heavenly Jerusalem as dreamed in the human imagination. Gothic artists were not clumsy craftsmen unable to grasp human anatomy or human visual perspective. They were servants of their faith, seeking to invent in their craftsmanship visions of a different and sacred world permeating this world and promising fulfillment in the world to come. The Renaissance became fascinated with the challenge to reproduce in stone or on plaster or canvas the clear copy of the retinal image, as if anticipating the art of photography. But behind this aim was a more powerful religious drive, namely, by artistic invention to raise the everyday reality to level of the ideal.

In baroque art following the high Renaissance and in its transitions to modern art, the role of the artist as an inventive visionary became more and more emphasized, whether with respect to the divine or the demonic, the beautiful or the grotesque. It may be that those of us who have lived through the twentieth century's artistic revolutions and agonized explorations in artistic forms are in a unique position to understand why art and craft, to be truly humble and respectful toward nature, must sometimes appear to distort nature and defy her seemingly harmonious rules. The artist both copies the world and invents it, showing what he or she has seen and dreamed.

We must not forget the element of play in all craft and art. Despite the necessity to respond to the so-called laws of nature, the craftsman artist, whether realistic or surrealistic, must play in order to invent. He or she is thus an example on the human scale of what Spinoza called *natura naturans* ("nature naturing"). Human play is but an extension—indeed a rather long extension—of what nature does all the time. Mother Nature goes to work under very flexible laws that leave room for the random. Nature does not plan the day for her children. She leaves them a bit loose within all their boundaries and instincts and waits to see what happens. Much of the resultant mutations are lethal, and these experiments die or at least become irrelevant to the ongoing drama. But some of them, by virtue of the good fortunes of random events, evolve into new, more complex, more creative forms.

The same is true of culture. No matter how rigid some of the rules may be, no matter how felicitous and successful any one school of any one artistic medium, all the arts and culture in general would die if it were not for their random, playful, courageous innovations. Furthermore, if innovation were a purely human trait, humanity would never have evolved in the first place. Any natural system intolerant of innovation and spontaneity could never have brought such a species as ours into being. But we did come into being and we continue to evolve. These facts alone point to a feature of prehuman nature that enabled the revolution that brought humanity into the natural world. Nature is a young, vibrant, and daring mother, risking all kinds of strangeness among her children, suffering cataclysms by virtue of her risk, but also earning delight by virtue of her inventiveness.

Leonardo da Vinci described humanity as the child of nature and art as humanity's child and nature's grandchild. Thus we and our arts and sciences have kinship with our environment. Just as tree leaves and snow crystals, wood grain and stone grain have endlessly varying patterns, so do the artifacts of human craft vary constantly, despite every rule of excellence or authority of fashion. Mother Nature, or as I prefer to say, Mother Earth, is a wonderful colony of natural and human devotees to craft, each fulfilling within its own sphere an endless round of variation. What we call human craft is but one version of a worldwide activity of the restless, nonrepetitive play of this whole breathing, growing, rolling globe.

What then distinguishes a work of fine art from the constant flow of human craftsmanship? What besides the ever-changing fashions of art schools and the art markets? Here I must confess my own religious biases. For me, any work of fine art must help me feel a cosmic dimension, if not steadily or frequently, at least from time to time and often when I am not looking for it. In other words, fine art must overlap with the aims of religion.

There is no precise way I know of defining the term *cosmic dimension*. If it were precise, it would be finite and therefore not cosmic. One can speak of it only obliquely in metaphors. Religion is itself composed of metaphors, mainly because the infinite by definition resists all measurement.

One cautious metaphor, derived from the writings of theologian Paul Tillich, has consistently proved useful to me. Tillich speaks of human experiences as occasionally pointing beyond themselves toward the infinite. He uses the phrase "a window on the Unconditional," not the Unconditional Itself, not a Thing in Itself, but a pointing toward it.

To be specific, imagine I am listening to a Bach prelude and fugue. It is wholly abstract in the sense that it calls up in my mind no specific image, no picture, no scenery or behavior. But I get the feeling this is what the world is like. The music begins with a basic theme or themes, connoting relatively stable elements in human experience. There is development, in that the themes do not remain the same. There is tension, in which the themes seem to fight for their own identity. There is transformation, in which the themes reach a higher level of complexity. There is reconciliation, in which the transformed themes unite in one voice. All this may not necessarily happen when I listen to Bach. But I may experience a cosmic vision, or rather, a cosmic listening, as though something vast that contains me is now contained within the humble limits of one piece of music, transferred by one artist's limited consciousness to the limited consciousness of his or her audience. Any work of fine art thus anticipates or replicates what is suggested by the Christian doctrine of incarnation: The cosmos mysteriously stoops to earth and allows itself to be enclosed in finite form of flesh.

The same cosmic dimension can occur in the theater. I remember such a moment in Shakespeare's *King Lear*. The King, who has been driven mad by the cruelty of his daughters, is wandering in the wilderness where he encounters the Duke of

Gloucester, another victim who is also wandering in the wilderness, having been brutally blinded by his enemies. The King, not recognizing his old friend Gloucester, recites to him a long catalogue of human sin, for which he finds prototypes in the lust and savagery of the natural world. Then, taking note that Gloucester cannot see, the King says:

> Look with thine ears...
> Thou has seen a farmer's dog bark at a beggar?
> ...And the creature run from the cur?
> There thou mightst behold the great image of authority: a dog's
>   obey'd in office.
> Thou rascal beadle, hold thy bloody hand!
> Why dost thou lash that whore? Strip thine own back,
> Thou hotly lusts to use her in that kind
> For which thou whip'st her...
> Through tatter'd clothes small vices do appear;
> Robes and furr'd gowns hide all.
> Plate sin with gold,
> And the strong lance of justice hurtless breaks;
> Arm it in rags, a pigmy's straw does pierce it.

Then in the next line the King fires a lightning bolt against any ultimate condemnation either of the poor sinner or the more sinful judge. He says,

> None does offend, none, I say none, I'll able 'em.
> Take that of me, my friend, who have the power
> To seal th' accuser's lips.

No situation or word in the New Testament describes so eloquently how from the depth of misery arises the power of universal judgment and universal forgiveness. Many times Shakespeare's enormous craft of language has brought tears of joy to my eyes. And in the lines just quoted, craft unites with a cosmic dimension to achieve the finest art. His art continues into yet another triumph when, immediately after this speech, Gloucester's son, Edgar, who is hidden nearby and pretending madness as a disguise

to save his own life, looks at the truly demented King and says as
an aside to the audience,

O, matter and impertinency mix'd.
Reason in madness!

To which I would add, clarity in ambiguity, justice in corrup-
tion, truth in confusion, light in darkness. For that is the way we
finite human beings look toward a cosmic dimension, always in
the midst of the local, limited, parochial lives we are destined to
live. Perhaps the greatest and strongest cosmic dimension in art
arises from the dimension of tragedy; tragedy seems to be the
medium for this kind of opening. While all is seemingly well and
the excellence of life is swelling the egos of the lords of power, the
sins of pride and prejudice are spreading the poison of their ivy
over land, vegetation, and houses. When they and their power,
when we and our powers are broken open by misfortune, it is possible though not inevitable that the larger truths of judgment and
forgiveness will shine in.

There is more to art than the biblical pattern of truth and redemption through suffering. I am reminded that the God-given
craft of a genius like Mozart is more often akin to the glory of
flowers and sunlight and pure running waters than to the tragic
Muse. Mozart and Schubert were true players of music, whose
play has the spontaneity of children and the complex ease of an
exquisitely trained athlete. Here is craft so simple and so mature
that it has the quality of ancient sun worship or of what St. Francis
worshipped in the clouds and all weather, the earth and her flowers. Such craft and art are descended from a long line of human
achievement and point beyond themselves to an inexhaustible future. The skill of Polynesian woodcarvers or of an ancient Greek
sculptor, the gestures of a Russian dancer or gymnast, a Japanese
flower arranger, a French chef, or a beloved spouse engaged in
some simple task—all these can show forth, beyond themselves,
the loveliness and ever-changing excellence of all creation. These

are the moments when the true music of life is heard. These are cornerstones on which life is built, benchmarks where truth and goodness are measured.

These high moments belong to a kind of angel choir that spans all time. They resonate with the distant past and join us with that past. They point toward a better future and thereby dignify whatever is good, true, and hopeful in the ambiguous present. Furthermore, they are possible on a small scale. They do not depend exclusively on wealthy museums, expensive theaters, and concert halls, nor are they limited to the few greatest geniuses in each artistic medium who happen to be living at any one time.

Craft is thus the mother of art as well as a universal quality in human nature and in that larger Nature upon which human nature depends. Let me offer one last small-scale example close to my own life and experience in which some of these larger claims for craft and art are more simply and intimately expressed.

Some time in the first half of the nineteenth century, the Howard Clock Company of Boston produced an eight-day wall clock, run by a weight, whose simple and elegant wooden cabinet was so shaped that this model was named the banjo clock. At one time these clocks were the standard classroom clocks for the public schools in Boston. Before I was born, my father, a jeweler in Boston, acquired three of these clocks at a time when they were being discontinued for use in the school system. He combined the best-preserved case with the best-quality movement, put them in shape, and mounted the clock in the home where he had brought the bride who was to be my mother. I do not know how old the clock is, but inside the case there is a sticker giving the name of a clock repairer in Boston written in ink, "Repaired, Feb. 1873." One hundred and two years later, in September 1975, I had that clock cleaned in Carbondale, Illinois. The mahogany case has a dark, satiny finish undamaged and even enhanced by time. The gold-leaf design on the glass front is still perfect. The clock face is bright and clear. The movement behind the eight-inch diameter face is no bigger than an orange, an economical and elegant assemblage of brass gears and a delicately hand-fashioned escapement. The clock does not keep perfect time, but near perfect. My clock is allowed those slight freedoms that are denied timepieces imprisoned in quartz and electricity.

I can remember two sounds from the clock back in the days of my childhood. There was the pleasant purring rasp of the winding mechanism, which my father alone was privileged to operate as once a week he lifted the weight to the top of its shaft. The other sound would sometimes come to me in the middle of the night. If I were to wake and go to the bathroom at the top of the stairs, I would hear all the way down in the front hall a comforting ticktock. In those days my hearing was acute. The true resonance of that tick-tock sound never returned to me in my adult years when, later in life, I inherited the clock for my family. Recently I was fitted with hearing aids. Then suddenly the precise difference between tick and tock sprang into my consciousness and reminded me of my childhood.

Thus the craftsmanship of that clock holds in miniature my model for all art and the influence of art upon religion. In that clock are the craftsmanship of unknown workers two centuries ago, my deceased father's skill and love, my childhood friend and comforter—a continuing presence in my youth, all returning their presences to my middle years and later, to my old age. It tells not only the moments of my day, but the days of my years. It teaches me to number my days that I may apply my heart unto wisdom. And I hope, when I have finally run down past any rewinding, my clock will be making the same music for one of my children and my children's children until they too are gathered to their fathers and mothers who went before them.

At the end of each week when I wind my clock, it is with tenderness and humility that I hope to express to this not-so-inanimate object the love and respect I feel for it.

Music and Wild Horses

Two of my favorite pictures hang on the walls of my home, one in my study and the other in the bedroom. The first is a modern reproduction of a medieval score of choral music. Each note of music is a little black square with the sides slightly concave. Its Latin text translates as follows:

Direct our feet into the path of peace, O God of Israel.
We bless thee.
Come, let us adore him, because he himself is our God.
Come, let us rejoice.

The ornamented border of this little piece of music is a trellis of flowers and arabesques dotted with amusing little figures of medieval musicians. One of them appears to be playing a harp; two of them squeeze medieval bagpipes; another scrapes his bow over a little vielle, the forerunner of the violin; and at the bottom a woman tootles away on a small portable pipe organ while a strange-hatted varlet pumps the bellows. Enclosed in the capital "C" at the beginning of the manuscript are three long-robed figures looking strangely Eastern and examining a musical score. Text and music dominate the page, and the musicians are locked into their rectangular frieze as securely as the faith and culture of the Middle Ages froze every person into a hierarchy of divinely ordained positions.

Apparently these medieval music makers had no difficulty with authority. Or if they did, they are not showing it. Quite the contrary, by their confined but lusty musicianship, they seem to be fulfilling the final injunction of the text: "Come, let us rejoice!"

The same "manuscript" is inscribed at the top with my own name and at the bottom with the name of a professor of music. It was a parting gift to me and many others like me who were four-year veterans of the Harvard Glee Club. We had voluntarily locked ourselves into a program of highly varied and demanding choral music, costing us a vast number of hours of rehearsal, traveling, and concert tours. We gave all our energy to the complete authority of our much-loved conductor, and all with no hint of any difficulty with authority. In fact, those four years of song were a rare combination of demanding labor and harmonious rejoicing. It may be that I am not oppressed by the rigid forms and odors of sanctity coming from the Middle Ages because I had once experienced in head and heart the exhilaration of responding to gifted musical authority, the authority of composers and the authority of a wise conductor.

Turn now from this carefully reserved picture of music-making to a small picture of wild horses. This second image is not a reproduction but an original, done on white paper in crayon with black, white, gray, and several brown tones shading into yellow. It is the size of a sheet of typewriter paper and is framed behind glass in a plain strip of red cedar with a natural finish. Against a neutral background, the artist has depicted a band of galloping wild horses, some of solid color and some pinto, racing from right to left across the picture plane. Very few of the horses are completely realized figures, either because they overlap one another or because they were purposely drawn so as to be only partly within the frame. Thus two pairs of legs and clattering hooves come down through the top border, while from below rears a horse head and windy mane, the rest of the body not yet arrived.

Long before I ever heard that Freud believed the horse to be a frequent symbol of our bodily drives, I could sense in this picture the plunging momentum and varying control of my own spirit, my own resistance to authority and love of novelty. Each horse is its own authority. Each is driven by a kind of irresistible inner ghost, its phantom pressures whitening the eye, flattening the ears, and rousing the hooves to thunder. Here is neither harmony nor the path of peace. For me, each animal has a kind of tragic cast: It plunges into its brief moment of life as seen through the window of the picture frame. Only for one cosmic instant is it its own master. Then it is maimed by transgression beyond the inexorable rectangle of the frame, and as it were, it disappears into the same darkness that had pushed it into life.

Shakespeare says the same thing about human beings in *As You Like It*:

> All the world's a stage,
> And all the men and women merely players:
> They have their exits and their entrances.

And what of the thoughtless and mortal fate of human players? Again Shakespeare, this time from *Measure for Measure*:

> ...man, proud man,
> Drest in a little brief authority,
> Most ignorant of what he's most assur'd,
> His glassy essence, like an angry ape,
> Plays such fantastic tricks before high heaven
> As make the angels weep; ...

But I should not present my wild horses to you in too somber or tragic a vein. They have a leap and life that is joyous. Besides, they were drawn by my youngest son when he was only eight or nine. I should not burden his blithe play with my melancholy glosses. He was having fun with his horses. The darker intimations of my years do not dim the luster of a child's vision of power and glory.

Also the fact remains that these two little works of folk art, the music manuscript and the wild horses, dwell in the same house. I wish it were always so in the heart of the man who looks at them and loves them and remembers. How I love harmony! How I relish that secure order, that tranquil music, which I bless by the name of peace or curse by the names of laziness, indolence, and inattention. Also, I crave excitement, nor have I lost with the passing of my younger years the perennial urge to knock down walls and to insult the face of propriety and ceremony. The horses speak to this darker self. All those inner dialogues about will I or won't I? Should I or shouldn't I? All those compulsively liberal attempts to balance freedom and order, innovation and conformity, impulse and judgment, anger and courtesy, often to the detriment of both sides of the dichotomy! This is the dilemma of every confirmed free person: We want to try everything under heaven but are frequently checked by the stoic admonition, "Nothing too much." I don't say this is a bad way to live. But I am reminded by my proud, joyous, and tragic horses, as well as by my humble and dedicated musicians, that this stoic compromise is not the only way to live and not always the best way.

I struggle with the fact that both pictures have a genuine place in one household. My walls do not say to the horses, "You shall not run," nor do they dilute or qualify the timeless relevance of the ancient Latin prayer for peace. Both pictures are there not to balance each other off as though each were dangerous without the countermotion of the other. Both pictures are there to fulfill the wall and to heal the often cloven heart of him who looks at them.

If I love my pictures, I have to go beyond the limits of reasonable balance. I must acknowledge that it is right for horses to leap, that the tragedy of their inevitable pain, decline, and death has nonetheless an inherent rightness in it. When Hamlet is oppressed by the rottenness in Denmark, when his life is plotted against and he feels his energies driving toward a tragic confrontation with the king, his trusted friend Horatio asks him to back off and bide his time. "You will lose, my lord," says Horatio. Hamlet replies,

> Not a whit, we defy augury; there's a special providence in the fall of the sparrow. If it be now, 'Tis not to come; if it be not to come, it will be now; if it be not now, yet it will come—the readiness is all.

"The Readiness Is All" is a good title for the wild horses picture. One has to be ready in the midst of one's own finitude, vulnerability, and inevitable death to respond with an answering leap to the whole glory and weight of life as it bears upon one's time and place and to know that someday each of us will lose it all.

But note that Hamlet can hold himself in readiness for death because of a faith that had its origin long before the Middle Ages and that was fulfilled within the Middle Ages: I refer to his paraphrase of Scripture, "There's a special providence in the fall of the sparrow." True, he must decide; he must act. But he has the sense of acting in a vast play whose producer and director provides wisely for the players. What appears to him as a risk also appears as belonging to an invisible harmony. "The readiness is all" applies also to the musicians, who in their quiet order sing out the notes prescribed to them without hesitation and, by their ready response, make a joyful noise unto the Lord.

Can we move beyond the point where our decisions are simply a balance of opposing ideals, beyond the nagging sense of mere stoicism? Certainly not always, but ideally, and at the right time, yes! We look for the courage to risk our security for something better. Perhaps the horse is a good symbol of that courage. It is not that horses are not fearful or anxious. The horse is largely a silent creature, standing in stillness and simplicity, keeping as slow and stately a rhythm as the movement of the sun, the day, and the night. But if you've been around them at all, you know how easily

they can be alarmed and how irrationally they will sometimes resist authority and control. Apparently their courage is not dimin-
ished by their fears as so often it is with us. It is one thing and a
natural thing to be afraid. But each must act, carrying fears right
in his or her teeth while moving through life.

Music has this kind of power. For music is no mere luxury or
casual pastime, no diversion from reality. It is rather a living power
joined with the power of life itself in all its moods. And the power
of music is conveyed both by dissonance and by harmony. In dissonance I feel the urge for change and the delight in forward
movement. In the orders of harmony, a strange and beautiful
transformation takes place; power becomes sweet, the leap and
energy of each separate musical line are brought into consonance
with all the others. What each musician does as an individual is
done for all. Their music played on separate contrasting instruments is like a conversation among different but equal persons.

Musicians know what it means to have a conductor, or in a
solo recital with piano or in a chamber group, to share conduct-
ing authority. They understand how their own conduct is not just
their own, but a motion within much wider surrounding motions,
a making of noise that makes music only if it is tuned to its own
larger structure of sound. There is a special providence in the fall
of a piano key and in the stroke of a bow, by whose authority the
musician is not compromised, but rather fulfilled.

I would not know quite how to view the many risks of life and
the final assurance of death if there were no sense of a special
providence, whether natural, or mythological, or both. This does
not mean that I or any people are uniquely favored by a divine
conductor to play out a neatly ordered life from the opening
measure to the final bar. I am called upon to improvise, to write
some of the score myself or interpret it freely, not simply to play
in a mechanical fashion what other people have written for me.
And this is good, the sight-reading and the free interpretation, the
composing of new parts and the rehearsing of a role that is given.

In this perspective the difference between the musicians and the wild horses diminishes. If the horse is wild, it is also programmed by a provident nature to a meaningful cycle of events. It is given not only to action but also to quiet, in which it stores up the energy for the next day's or the next measure's effort. And when musicians submit to daily practice and run up and down their monotonous exercises, they do so for the sake of freedom, for that moment when they pass beyond mere technique to a language uniquely expressive of their own selfhood, their own heights and depths. The score may come from Bach or Beethoven; the music in its best moments is as fresh as the morning, never before heard or felt in just that way.

In his Norton Lectures given at Harvard some years ago, one of the most innovative composers of the twentieth century, Igor Stravinsky, states:

> My freedom consists in my moving about within the narrow frame that I have assigned myself for each of my undertakings. I shall go even further: my freedom will be so much the greater and more meaningful the more narrowly I limit my field of action and the more I surround myself with obstacles. Whatever diminishes constraint diminishes strength. The more constraint one imposes, the more one frees oneself of the chains that shackle the spirit.
>
> —*Poetics of Music in the Form of Six Lessons*

I believe Bach could have written the same paragraph. Bach is the great expresser of truths fashioned out of the lives most of us live. He holds their counterpoint within an overriding harmonic pattern. By virtue of these very confinements and loose ends, he found the freedom of his genius.

Now that I have reached what some have euphemistically called the sunset years, I am reminded that all pieces of music, like every life, must come to an end. And the more beautiful the music, the more one must have a sense of regret as one feels its irresistible cadences moving toward their final rest. This points to an ultimate mystery, if ever any mystery were ultimate: the urge in each of us to live forever and the total inability to imagine forever, much less achieve it.

How differently great composers have come up to that mystery! Bach did not seem to worry about the double bar at the end. When he came to it, he just stopped with little more than a slight retard. Then he went on to the next work. Beethoven, by contrast, did not go gently into the good night of the double bar. The famous Fifth Symphony is a perfect example of a work whose ending coda refuses to end, but goes wildly crashing on as if death needed to be defied with yet another blow on the kettle drums. Mozart stands in between Bach and Beethoven, both chronologically and in style and philosophy. His endings are truly final, but generally more gentle and modest, almost as though he were anticipating his own premature and nontriumphant death.

Some deaths do have a kind of Beethoven-esque agony or triumph, while others look as abrupt and necessary as Bach's endings. Still others have a modest sweetness about them like Mozart's ending measures. But how any death feels to the dying person we shall never know until we get there, and even then may not know at all what is happening. In any case, we shall not be able to convey whatever we may learn in our last moments to those who are left behind.

Poet Gerard Manley Hopkins knew a majestic and powerful blacksmith named Felix Randal who was inexorably reduced to a premature death by a crippling illness. And Hopkins addresses the final lines of his poetic tribute to his friend's memory in this way:

> Thy tears that touched my heart, child, Felix, poor Felix Randal
> How far from then forethought of, all thy more boisterous years
> When thou at the random grim forge, powerful amidst peers,
> Didst fettle for the great gray drayhorse his bright and battering sandal!
>
> —"Felix Randal"

The leap of courage and the musical stillness that points beyond all action, all invention, all expression, are thus indispensable elements to any fulfilled life. The fact that they both belong and that neither is logically reconciled to the other must be accepted, digested, incorporated into that ongoing movement we call life. In their entrances and exits, the wild horses have their episodes of joy even as they run toward their inescapable end. Perhaps they also have some kind of equine music that they alone can hear, some sounding stillness that enriches their long hours of standing still. I know that we have such music in the human species, that we can be brought to a musical attentiveness that transcends whatever else we think ought to be done, attended to, or savored.

In the music that touches us the most deeply, wherever or however it comes to us, we may find an ultimate reconciliation of the leap of life with the final stillness of life. In the very vivacity of music, we are invited, "*Venite, exultemus,*" "Come, let us rejoice." In the solemnity of music with its frequent rests, we find ourselves guided in the "paths of peace." How important it is to do something worth doing and to do it well! How equally important it is to do nothing and to recognize thereby the ultimate quiet toward which each of us is tending. The same Hamlet who looked toward death with the courage of a war horse by saying to Horatio, "The readiness is all," a few hours later, falling mortally wounded, says to the same Horatio his last words: "The rest is silence." Neither Shakespeare nor I made or make any claim to know what it means to the dying person to die. But this I can affirm without hesitation: The effect upon me of this classic death scene in Shakespeare's *Hamlet* is to lead me to the path of peace.

With Gerard Manley Hopkins, I pray,

Elected Silence, sing to me
And beat upon my whorlèd ear,
Pipe me to pastures still and be
The music that I care to hear.

—"The Habit of Perfection"

Superstition, Doubt and Faith

THE GREEK WORD *muthos*, which our word *myth* comes from, means anything delivered by word of mouth—a conversation; a speech; a story, tale, or narrative; a fable or legend; a history either true or fabulous. There is general agreement today that the word *myth* connotes a fictitious story, a tale that could not be literally true. But since these stories were once so widely believed, not only by the Greeks but also by their successors in world power, the Romans, one must admit that they were once useful, if now no longer true.

I have visited Delphi three times. During one of these visits I seemed to have encountered Apollo. This encounter was useful to me without making me a devotee of the deity, certainly without making me believe in the literal reality of the god.

There are many often contradictory myths purporting to give a "history" of Apollo. He was born on the small Aegean island of Delos, the son of Zeus and Leto. One body of myths holds that Leto was the original wife of Zeus. Others say that Hera, commonly recognized as Zeus's wife, came first and that Zeus's union with Leto aroused a fierce jealousy in Hera, who dispatched a monster named Pytho to pursue and kill Leto. She escaped from Pytho long enough to give birth to Apollo, who in turn became a skilled archer. He succeeded in giving ultimate protection to his mother by shooting Pytho near what is now the Greek town of Delphi. The god left the huge Pythian carcass there to rot, thereby giving to Apollo the epithet Pythian and the original name of Pytho to what is now Delphi. Apollo ranged through the nearby mountain mass of Parnassus, where he fathered twelve daughters—the nine Muses, patronesses of the arts, and the three Graces, patronesses of feminine beauty. The reputation of Apollo became increasingly favorable: He was considered god of the sun, a skilled hunter, also a mathematician who understood the mysteries of music and measurement, and finally, a source for prophecies of the future. This function of prophecy led Apollo to found the sacred shrine of Delphi, where his priestesses gave oracles to thousands of petitioners seeking to know their fate.

In Delphi is a lovely clear natural fountain of water that involves another love-death miracle. A maid, Castalia, caught the eye of Apollo, who tried to ravish her. She leaped into the fountain and died before Apollo could reach her. Because he had caused Castalia's death, Apollo consecrated the spring in her name, and ever after this crystalline stream has been called the Castalian spring. He promised that pilgrims who bathed in the Castalian spring and drank its pure water might receive from the Muses the poetic gift. Thus the wisdom of the Delphic oracle and the inspiration of the Castalian spring, situated side by side in Delphi, caused this town to become a favorite place of pilgrimage in the ancient world.

I visited the Castalian spring before dawn one morning, before any other tourists had arrived. I found its waters flowing from a huge cleft in the mountain wall and following an ancient man-made channel of hewn stone. The channel is about eighteen inches wide and the flow about three inches deep, as clear and pure as the finest snow-fed alpine stream in our own Rocky Mountains. I lay face down on a small flat stone bridge over the stream, washed my face and hands, and then cupped in my hands some of the pure water to drink. As I drank I spoke in my mind a little prayer to Apollo, asking for the poetic gift as is the custom. Even as I was swallowing the water of the Castalian spring, the god answered me with these straightforward sentences: "You don't need an extra gift. It is up to you to perfect what gifts you already have." I started to chuckle, believing that my own mind was being critical of my own prayer. Again the god seemed to intervene, interrupting my quiet chuckle, by causing my eyeglasses to fall into the water. As I fished them out, a message more like an oracle came to me from Apollo: "If you want the poetic gift, learn better how to see." The truth came home to me that prayers do not always deserve to be answered, that sometimes prayers are properly answered by being corrected.

I got up on my feet and walked cheerfully away, wrapped in a fine and gentle euphoria.

Several months later, I took part in a theological discussion at the Collegium gathering on Cape Cod, a group consisting of liberal ministers and theologians. In order to make the point that faith and unfaith can be mysteriously mingled, I told them my Apollo story. I argued that I do not worship Apollo and had no genuine faith that the Castalian spring could make any difference in my life. And yet, the bathing, the drinking, and the prayer seemed appropriate in that place. And what came of it was a new enlightenment, an enrichment not as I had prayed, but much better, as I was answered.

Immediately, an old friend who has always been a courteous theological adversary took the floor. He is Khoren Arisian, one of the brightest, best read, most articulate of liberal ministers. He is also an unadulterated, pure, foursquare humanist with a strong lance against any kind of theological hypothesis or opinion. Khoren wasted no time interpreting my so-called encounter with Apollo. No god ever founded the place, he said; no god ever endowed it with traditions; no god spoke to me. Parnassus is rock; Castalia is water. The sole source of my prayer and of every so-called answer was my own mind. I took nothing away from the Castalian spring that I had not brought with me. From beginning to end, I was speaking to myself, as any liberal would quickly recognize. Khoren did not say this loudly or belligerently. He was repeating in a friendly fashion what he had been saying to me for years. And I half believed him. Certainly I had no grounds to prove that he was wrong.

Now let me tell you what he said to me after the meeting. "You've been to Delphi three times?"

"Yes," I answered.

His head shaking, "Lucky guy! I've been there only once, but I am going again this spring. Don't you agree that it is one of the most beautiful places in the world?"

"Yes," I replied. "From what little I have seen of the world, it is one of the great wonders."

He went on, "You know, I can't think of a more profound source of religious inspiration than Delphi. All those skilled people who brought their human art and beauty to Delphi's natural beauty. Thanks for your story; I intend to get up early and bathe in the Castalian spring." I came close to tears as I shook hands with my old fencing partner and saw once more the clean beauty of the free church.

Many years ago in Chicago I had a happy psychoanalysis with an analyst named Morris Sklansky. I remember the day when the whole period of my visits with him suddenly seemed to come to an end. In a way I did not want to leave him because I honored his kind and gentle services to me. I asked the doctor for one more appointment so that he could review for me his understanding of the stages of my analysis. He politely turned me down with this little sentence: "No need. I don't know anything about you that you don't know yourself." This suggested to me that what has always been called salvation is really a private transaction of one mind with itself and that to attribute salvation to a god or a doctor is superstitious.

I had discovered a great deal about myself in psychoanalysis with the doctor's help—not even one doctor's help, because my doctor had been trained by other doctors, some of whom had been trained by Sigmund Freud, who had in turn been versed in rich cultures going back to ancient Greece and beyond. There was in this whole history not one point that could serve as the true origin of my well-being. Nor could any psychiatrist, old or new, explain the precise mechanics of how those many doctor-patient conversations resulted in my being healed. Psychiatry has certain scientific theories, but its success depends mainly upon its artistry. And what is successful art but that deep and rich well-doing and well-being the Greeks once attributed to Apollo and the Muses?

The day may come when psychiatric healing is understood more quantitatively and mechanistically, in terms of chemistry and physics within the brain. But as of the present moment, there are no such hypotheses, much less proof as to how mind healing works. Is it the achievement of a brilliant physician? Is the patient self-healed? Or does the combination of doctor, patient, plus medical and cultural tradition work a mysterious miracle, a work of art? I incline toward the last-named alternative. Dr. Sklansky and I talked about my life as a person and my calling as a minister and theologian. These, much more than the principles of Freudian analysis, were our major themes. Thus the deep layers of my life and trade were mined for their relevance to the present day. My doctor was not a doctrinaire preacher of the Gospel of Freud (although he took many opportunities to honor his patron saint). Mainly he led me to talk about what I knew, or thought I knew, not about his expertise.

Thus I conclude that it is superstitious to say "My doctor healed me." It is also superstitious to brag, "I healed myself." The truth of the matter—as near as I can come to it—is that human art, combined with the natural graces of the human body, lodged in the ancient wisdoms of human culture, and seated finally in the ancient dignity of the earth itself—all these came to a head mysteriously in the time of my healing.

Thus we are led back to the long lines of pilgrims threading their way past the huge crags of Parnassus to the mountain shelf and seat of Pythian Apollo at Delphi. I see them, their graceful, many-colored robes glinting in the noonday sun or richly glowing by torchlight, as they mounted the Sacred Way toward Apollo's shrine. A quarter mile away they had washed in Castalia's spring. As they walked, their road was flanked by gorgeous statuary in marble and bronze. They take note of the special treasuries, like little temples, built by particular cities to house their gifts to the god. They admire the vast polygonal wall, a miracle of tight-fitting, unmortared stone supporting the whole weight of the temple. They turn and turn again until they approach, chanting, the seat of the oracle and bow before her steaming tripod and the magic of her somber voice.

Let us question them as Socrates might on the nature of their faith. Did your bath in the Castalian spring make you truly eloquent and divinely pure? Of course not, they answer, that is superstition. Yet how can we approach the god without the bath as a tangible gesture of hoped for purity or without a spoken prayer for wisdom, art, and purity? Did the sibyl answer your queries and quandaries about the future? Certainly not, that would be sheer superstition. Yet in the very ambiguities of what she spoke we are now encouraged to hope and work for triumph, or if such is not to be, to accept the tragedy that darkly looms within her words. Have you fully rewarded Apollo for his grace by a gift deposited in your city's treasury? We? Reward Apollo? We have contributed to the priests, their livelihood, yes, their wealth. What does Apollo need of our poor gifts? It is superstition to claim to feed or clothe or flatter the immortal god. Yet how can we come to this place and go away once more if we have made no sacrifice? This ground is holy, and all who walk thereon must dress, and pray, and speak, and listen, and give, and sacrifice as the ancients, as both gods and humans have commanded.

In the midst of this imagined dialogue, an ancient Jewish saying comes to mind: "Blessed art thou, O Lord our God, who sanctifiest us by thy commandments." It is superstition to think that a ritual act makes one pure and holy. But the sense of commandment, the sense of obligations to the ancestors, their loves and their deaths, and to children yet unborn—such commandments put us on the way to holiness, on the way to wisdom, on the way to fulfillment. The fulfillments of holiness and wisdom, if they exist at all, are in the life lived, in our own doing, in the doings of others, and in the strivings of causes and powers within us extending back beyond the memory of humanity to the beginnings of space, time, and substance. Meanwhile we are sanctified, that is, called to holiness and put on the way to holiness, by at the least paying attention to the commandments the culture and its god have ordained.

None of us knows where we leave off and our environment begins. None of us can determine a sharp line between personal achievement and the influences both good and bad of other persons and the deeper interpersonal layers of our environment. When you use your native speech to sing a song, it is your song and it is also some ancient voice over which you have no control, coming to life within you.

It is superstitious to exalt any one element in this exquisitely composite drama and say this is the cause of it all. Such arbitrary selections are not holy; rather, they are the idols that proud men and women ignorantly and superstitiously worship. To worship the human mind is no less superstitious than to believe that Apollo can awaken the mind to poetry. To worship the human race is analogous to the Greek habit of calling their race superior to all the rest, superior to the "barbarians." The races of our animal ancestors prepared the way for us, gave to our bodies the instinctive and automatic mechanisms by which all living creatures guard their health and perpetuate their kind. We have finally learned that our superiority to the other animals is partial, that in some respects they surpass us. We need them more than they need us. Certainly the whole earth needs them as a part of the vast non-human program for terrestrial health. We need a good earth as the indispensable condition of our own good health. Yet to worship the earth, or the sun, or the solar system upon which the earth depends would be superstitious. As people holding joint citizenship with animals, plants, the planet, and our native star, we are all worshippers of the mysterious and secret unity of which the intergalactic wonders of creation have sprung. We have only the slightest knowledge of that fullness we worship.

Our knowledge, shadow of a shadow, is so vague that I cannot blame anyone who refuses to worship at all. There is a sense in which the worship of the whole, while less idolatrous than the worship of a part, is still superstitious. This reality puts every religious person in a dilemma: On the one hand, there is the need for worshipful celebration, out of the manifold revelations of love that extend through humanity to its environment and cosmos. On the other hand, one cannot understand how a cosmos can hear, or grasp, or respond to human praise and prayer. The human spirit begs the human voice to sing praise. The human mind asks, What's the use? Love creates the song. Our critical intelligence denies the efficacy of singing. Thus faith and unfaith live in all of us. Faith would not be faith were it not challenged by doubt.

No church can or should force any person's decision, especially one who is caught between faith and doubt. Our faiths differ, as do their corresponding doubts, and in recognition of these differences, the love we bear to one another must transcend our differences. It is just in that transcending love that I affirm the liberal church, that I will not yield to the blandishments of more positive believers or think that I need strengths and defenses more than I need my own.

It is also in the strength of that love that I present and announce my kinship with the generations before me who have sung their praise and offered their sacrifices. I affirm holy places, holy cities, holy pieces of ground. I take into loving remembrance and lively visitation certain great shrines of faith that exert their spirit to arouse my own, sharing in the midst of reasonable doubt a faith that could not be mine if there were no visible, audible, and tangible reminders of it. Thus, in the chances and changes of life's history, I gather to myself certain real and experienced phenomena, certain biblical words and other poetry, certain natural occurrences and cultural achievements. These are all reminders of human love, devotion, and sacrifice, held over beyond the deaths of their originators, blessing me in this latter day, as I hope someday some few of my descendants will be blessed by actions I will have achieved now and left behind me when my person is gone and my name is forgotten.

Finally, in the name of all the communion of the doubting faithful, men and women and their animal and vegetable ancestors, in the name of rocks, sand, water, sun, wind, and stars that preceded the birth of life, and in the name of the great universe that is itself dying and yet will be reborn, I offer my own small voice sounding in deep and grateful praise. Psalm 104 speaks for my faith and echoes my doubts in one beautiful line: "I will sing to the Lord as long as I live; I will sing praise to my God while I have being."

The rest is silence.

Living Religion and a Liberal Tradition

To be liberal in religious life, to be oriented to novelty and experiment, is not incompatible with a deep respect for ancient religious traditions. Freedom and tradition are complementary. The care with which religious liberals exercise and transmit their tradition should strengthen their aptitude for intellectual inquiry and bring more sharply into play their powers of analytical precision and creative improvisation.

The primary role of tradition in any culture is the ordering and articulation of experience. Language itself is perhaps the most basic of all traditions. Its forms and meanings are given, although not in so rigid a fashion that no originality can emerge. There is a definiteness to any language that commands attention and respect if meaningful communication is to occur. In the power of that formal definiteness, people articulate to one another and within themselves something of the complexity of meaning inherent in the variety of their experiences. There should be no need to belabor the point that language would fail utterly in its function—would not exist—if it did not carry with it traditional images and traditional rules of usage and procedure by which a community of communication is established. The most skeptical philosopher insisting that one define terms carefully and use them consistently is appealing not to a principle of freedom but rather to a principle of linguistic tradition. Two or more discussants must share what is traditionally given in their words before they can profitably weigh the significance of their words.

The same is true of the religious life—especially true since the objects of religious devotion are often difficult to define. Here we must depend upon more than linguistic traditions since our normal framework of linguistic meaning is scarcely adequate to the task of theological articulation. Only when language is supplemented by expressive traditions in art and worship is articulation (and thereby, communication) achieved. People must literally help one another to religious realization by communal use of the cultural tools inherited for that purpose. And their powers of novel realization will be consequent upon, not separate from, their mastery of the given articulations of their culture.

The vital thread of traditional expression in the arts is perhaps not adequately acknowledged in this age of artistic innovation. In "The Language of Poetry," Northrop Frye points out that the history of literary art shows a continuing preoccupation with archetypal images of the human condition. Literary creativity is not purely a fresh response of writers to the stimuli of their own times. It is rather a wrestle for significant novelty within inherited forms of literary expression and subject matter. Frye notes a parallel with the religious life in which the myths and rituals of a given culture carry the archetypal models providing the means by which the people of that culture articulate to one another their basic religious questions. Meanings of any great significance are far too complex in their social and communal bearing to be generated *de novo* by the isolated individual. The natural liberal tendency to say, "Each person must achieve his or her own religious faith" makes sense only against the broad background of inherited tradition. The very opportunity to choose what one will believe limits one's freedom of judgment to the few vivid and viable alternatives given in one's own time and place. Even before any sensible choice can be made, there is a prior and more fundamental task facing the individual of articulating internally what some of the choices and questions are, where to begin, and especially, where one is standing while one begins.

There is a danger that these elemental tasks will be construed in too intellectual a fashion, as though a lecture about the meaning of worship were a valid substitute for its living experience. Works of art and religious liturgies are not propositional arguments to be constantly weighed critically but living actions commending their truths with the persuasive force of experienced fact. Their very vitality and power of persuasion can raise intellectual questions and lead to study and analysis. But total involvement at the experiential level precedes and stimulates theoretical detachment, not vice versa.

The subject matter of religious articulation is theoretically not bound to any one time and place. But practically speaking it is more difficult to appropriate an alien religious tradition than to assimilate one that has already helped determine one's own culture and experience. The religious and intellectual traditions of Israel and Greece and their joining under the Christian aegis have been decisive in the formation of Western religious culture. It is reasonable to expect that these traditions continue to provide the images and archetypes for the liberal's questioning and thinking. Our traditions are not dogmas in and of themselves; they are simply our native religious language. The real value of this language in comparison to alternatives can best be estimated only after we have learned to speak it well. In this respect, the liberal church has a primary and truly basic task: It has to present via the media of ritual, drama, story, and artistic celebration the particular images of religious encounter and religious hope that belong to the Hellenic and Judeo-Christian traditions. Raw experience is a mystery that persistently eludes our powers of expression. It is a fire burning within the individual, ever seeking some outlet, desiring communicative expression and self-definition. One's church should be the first place in one's life where something of the richness, the terror, and the ultimate hopes of the human condition are articulated. Articulations may occur as questions or answers, doubts or affirmations. But such articulations occurring in the setting of the church, as in the arts, are not to be presented or construed primarily as propositional arguments awaiting testing and verification. Rather they are ritual, dramatic, musical, or narrative occasions in which essential meanings are offered through the very form and immediacy of the media. They are actions and reenactments primarily, and only secondarily ideas and hypotheses.

The unique function of the church lies in its acts of worship. People seek together to commune directly with those realities that they believe sustain their lives and give meaning to their existence. To substitute analysis and discourse for worship is to miss the religious moment and compromise the very character of the church.

The preservation and presentation of traditional forms and ideas of worship ensure that there shall be definite articulation of religious feeling and not an endless and unfulfilled groping. This task is not to be construed as antiquarian. The past is never alive except in relation to contemporary experience. The past comes into the present only as it provides a resonance for an activity, feeling, and stimulus occurring contemporaneously. The musical metaphor is singularly apt. The intensity of current events may cause people's feelings to vibrate as the strings of a musical instrument. They will vibrate rapidly but with a thin and pathetic sound, with difficult strainings, unless these motions of time and circumstance occur in relation to some resonance chamber of the past. The arts and the church provide the inherited yet malleable shapes of cultural resonance chambers. The church will sound most richly when it is not stuffed either with rigid dogmas from the past or with the complex fragments of contemporary experience. The time-tested shape of the sound chambers of any good musical instrument is traditional. These shapes lend resonance and tonality to whatever contemporary event may move through its chambers. The church's newest concerns are treasured no less than its oldest memories, but the treasuring of either old or new is dependent upon their mutual coexistence.

Such a view of the church recognizes the psychological value of relating the individual to a broad community of the living and the dead. One is lifted out of the isolating belief that one's ecstasies and agonies are unique and related solely to an immediate location in time and space. One is put into a relationship at once historical, concrete in time, and eternal, essential, and beyond time.

Thus, while the church is also a house of study, a place of inquiry, it is primarily a house of worship. Worship is its most native emphasis; intellectual analysis is always consequent upon the reality of its worship, never a substitute for it. The dramatic and celebrative element should dominate and the element of inquiry should be secondary.

We are speaking here of emphases, not of mutually exclusive functions. It is my contention that the habit of critical analysis is most readily stimulated when the celebrative and ritual functions of the church are kept fresh and imaginative, when they are not allowed to atrophy by unbroken repetition. The mind is awakened by the deepening of the feelings and dulled by the failure to touch the depth of feeling. In this respect the arts are primary tools and allies of living religion, and the very health of the intellect is dependent upon the vigor of the arts working through the realm of worship.

To be in the church, to preach or receive its sermons, and to join in its worship is to participate in a definite spiritual heritage. To be in a liberal church is also to be free with respect to that heritage—free to appropriate what appears to be its contemporary relevance and free to raise questions and to rule out what appears to be irrelevant. In all that I have said about tradition, I presuppose its liberal transmission. I assume that religion should not be bound in a fixed dogma, but should possess the continuing energy to search for new ways and new expressive forms. The reformation must continue. It should be based on a spiritual substance that underlies and stimulates all our free probings and supports us when we fail as well as when we succeed. In the interplay between heritage and freedom, we discover the meaning of the liberal transmission of tradition.

The biblical heritage is not a single creed demanding belief but a challenge to all who seek religious affirmation. There is a solid core to this challenge, and there are contrasting elements surrounding it. At the core is a group of poems, speeches, and stories in which the whole of creation is understood as under the lordship of a power at once loving and merciful toward all creatures and yet far transcendent over the grasp of any creature including the wisest among us. It is a vision in which the mystery and austerity of the Greek or tragic outlook have a place. But in the biblical traditions there are also visions of hope, exaltation, and trust. It is a vision involving the metaphor of person-to-person transactions with the depth of being.

The liberal church does not require a literal adherence to the Scriptures. The Bible is not one pure strain of religious witness, but a composite of affirmations and denials of divine glory and human worth, divine judgment and human fallibility. We need to broaden the conception of what is *biblical* to include our Hellenic heritage in our religious attitudes. Although we have not inherited directly from Greece any modes of worship that we can easily assume, we have her art, her drama and literature, and her philosophy as reminders of deep and lasting cultural forms. Her celebration of natural beauty, her rationalism, her sense for the tragic, and her stoical courage are all part of what for many centuries has been held as *classical* in Europe and North America. The self-trust and communal hopes of the liberal, which are deeply fortified by the biblical heritage, are ever challenged by the tragic humanism of our Greek heritage and its occasional counterparts in the Bible. The biblical anchorage of hope is not untroubled and should never claim to be. But the fact remains that the great gift of the biblical heritage lies bright before our eyes, preserved and transmitted, however imperfectly, through the living church. It represents the communion of those diverse and often conflicting believers who have been touched by its haunting challenge, who have made some of its ways their ways, who have adopted some of its prayers, and who have taken one another in marriage, christened their children, and been received at their death under its many blessings.

The objective and historical core of biblical faith is constantly in dialogue with changing times, just as everyone carries on an inner dialogue between his/her own biographical past and the unfolding present. If that dialogue takes place with vigor, both one's present and one's past, one's modern existence and religious heritage are transformed and renewed. The liberal church trusts that its heritage is a continuing challenge to haunt the human spirit, especially in its great narratives of the life and death of Jesus. Here and elsewhere we are challenged to come to terms with these models even if the "coming to terms" is largely negative. As long as one's rejections are carefully considered, occurring by reason of deep experience and soul searching rather than by a swift and careless parochial bias, such persons help the church to achieve its functions in a fully significant way. And even if the reality of God in many people's lives has grown dim or has vanished altogether, still the dramatic witness of the church's heritage and substance must be available to all without coercion. Thus one is free to make decisions more meaningfully and generously than in the atmosphere of a narrower liberalism where the classic questions are never raised.

I am bold to counsel the leaders of the liberal church—ministers and laypersons and certainly those who teach our children—to be mindful of their obligation. Their own personal tastes and decisions relating to theological matters are unimportant compared with their duty as guardians of an ancient institution. They must make available to future generations that basic Jewish and Christian substance from which the power of the church has arisen. They are also under obligation to broaden the conception of heritage by relating the church's life to nonbiblical sources of spiritual insight. They are free to teach and celebrate more than the Bible; they are not free to teach and celebrate less.

Finally it should be said that no doctrine or body of teaching is in itself an automatic guarantee of virtue. An atheist may be ethically more acute and socially more productive than a believer. This fact proves neither the validity of unbelief nor the fallacy of belief. People differ in their powers as well as in their beliefs. They must be helped to feel free to believe even though a more acute and admirable person does not. There can be no promise that "if you believe as I do, your life will be like mine." Religion is an art, not a technique. There are good people and weak, righteous and evil in every church and outside every church. And in all people measures of goodness and evil are paradoxically mixed. We must ever remind ourselves that the penetration of grace is an utterly mysterious event that no person or church controls and that can fail the instant either persons or churches claim to know its secret.

In short, we cannot conclude that because wonderful people live apart from the spiritual substance of the church, the church is irrelevant. The substance of the heritage is given to us who care for the church as a trust to be guarded, reformed, transformed, and transmitted. It demands that we be honest and free with ourselves and our neighbors, openly confessing our doubts as well as our assurances. It demands that we bring to bear in our religious pilgrimages anything good or true or beautiful that we happen to find in or outside the tradition. The final issue of all our religious efforts is happily not ours to decide.

Myth and the Modern World

THE MYTHOLOGIES of the Bible are part of our religious and cultural heritage. For many, the Bible represents literal history. For others, it is a humanly constructed avenue to religious faith and religious truth. Yet we now live in the age of science, in which mythical materials are considered false and unwholesome for the health of civilization. It is important to ask what is the philosophic basis for treating myths in this fashion, especially at a time when fundamentalist religions, whether Jewish, Christian, or Muslim, are demanding literal adherence to the details of the Bible or the Koran. Although science-oriented people have struggled against fundamentalism in recent centuries, the Western episodes of this battle between reason and myth have been taking place at least as long as early Greek civilization. We do not ask a new question when we ponder the uses of myth in an age of science.

Why, in this time when scientific standards are predominant, do so many people insist on basing their beliefs on myths? I think we must recognize that most people live and die with feelings of limitation and yearnings for transcendence. It is safe to define *Homo sapiens* as a species far less sapient than they would like to be, also far less able. Beyond what passes for knowledge is a huge abyss of mystery. Beyond all fullness there is always hunger; beyond satisfaction, desire; beyond righteousness, guilt; beyond life, death. We know of no species so sensitive to finitude and so impatient to transcend it as we are. As a consequence of human finitude, human beings also live by intuiting and projecting transcendence models. The most common and most communal method for pursuing transcendence is religion. The most common tools of religion are the telling of myths and the reenactment of these myths in the worship of some kind of divine transcendence model or agency.

Twentieth-century scholar Mircea Eliade describes how in all early religions, their principal use of myth is to transcend the "terror of time." Time is the measure of decay, and the whole world is caught in time's irresistible drive toward nonbeing. Parallel to and transcendent over the expected tragedies of history and the decay of all things through time, religions envision some area of perfection and fulfillment or at least some power of renewal after the ravages of time. This is the realm of the gods, or God, the immortal ones with their prototypical dramas of eternal goodness and value. Ritual is the common medium for a religious community to achieve periodic identification with the divine realm leading to periodic refreshment of the temporal realm. Myth is the story in oral or written form of archetypal events, which rituals reenact. By this means the people, the tribe, and even the earth are believed to be renewed, thereby transcending the terror of time. Furthermore, these myths and rituals give not only a future hope but also a present way of living. They are divine prototypes of conduct with respect to every significant aspect of life. Thus myth and ritual confirm a primal history, enunciate a crucial religious vision and faith, and declare the foundations for an extensive law and art.

What does a transcendence model purport to transcend? It transcends time, for it is a program still to be fulfilled and yet treasured as being even now in the process of fulfillment. It transcends verification, for it is a faith continually tested and yet extending in principle beyond all verifying activity. It could be falsified and eventually might lose its imperial position. But falsification would never occur by virtue of a single exception. On the contrary, only a deadly flood of exceptions protracted over a long period of time without the occasional refreshment of a single encouraging event would drive the faithful person to admit falsification. As long as a few lifelong habits of thought persist and as long as a few supporting instances can be experienced, the faith survives.

By the term *transcendence model* I do not mean to refer only to a mystical reality understood by esoteric means. Rather, I wish to connote a certain sense of Reality (with a capital "R") serving as both the container and contrasting foil into which and against which all relativities and partial realizations of human perception and knowledge are projected. For Einstein, the transcendence model would be the Ultimate Order toward which all our scientific and humanistic probabilities approach. For Tillich, it would be "the Unconditional," "the God beyond the God of theism." In each case we would be dealing with what Schelling called *das Unvordenkliche*, "that before which thought cannot penetrate." Such models are transcendent in the sense that they are not justified in terms of any prior reasons or discernible causes, but are affirmed in their own right as the ultimate ground of being as well as the ultimate limit of human understanding.

One feature of the history of the West is that it has gradually demythologized its discourse by converting mythical transcendence models (concrete narratives of gods and humans) into abstract transcendence models (general principles underlying systems of thought). Thus theology gives way to philosophy. Despite this process, scraps of myth remain even in modern discourse. In many respects a more concrete, narrative-style transcendence model may be better suited to modern sensibilities than abstract transcendence models. In short, demythologizing has proceeded far enough. Now may be the time, even while guarding critical intelligence, to consider remythologizing.

THE GREEK TRANSCENDENCE MODEL

In his *The Theology of the Early Greek Philosophers*, Werner Jaeger has documented in impressive detail the gradual shift from the mythological to the philosophic mind. He describes a long history of reconstructing mythical tales and images into abstract and universal principles. After several generations of gradual demythologizing, Plato emerged as a highly sophisticated rationalist who achieved an almost complete transition from *mythos* to *logos*, from myth to reason. Plato sought to rule mythological tales out of the ideal state and its educational system and to substitute a thoroughgoing deductive thought system, a system proceeding from the archetypes of reason to a judgment over the relative value and meaning of all the objects of sensory experience. Yet he was not able to cleanse of all myth the world of thought that he inhabited; nor could he bring to completion the anti-mythical trend begun by his predecessors. I refer not only to his use of specific myths in some of his dialogues (*Phaedrus*, *The Republic*, and *Timaeus*), but also to the mythical components at the heart of his seemingly rational nonmythical transcendence model. Having been influenced by Pythagoras (as well as the Orphic myths that are woven into Pythagorean religion), he affirmed the reality of a realm of divine and immortal perfection expressed in terms of Unity, or The One. The One (a noncorporeal realm or entity) held within it all the *essences*, or perfect models, of how reality should be understood rationally. He believed this transcendent realm to be the true source and ultimate destiny of the human immortal soul. True reasoning leads, so Plato thought, toward the ultimate release of any human immortal soul from the bondage of its flesh into a perfectly good and unchanging divine realm.

The nature of Plato's transcendence model—The One—is critical for understanding much of Western thinking, including scientific thinking. Its key characteristic is the image of changelessness in contrast to the ravages and terrors of ordinary time and change: "Everything which is good, whether made by art or nature or both, is least liable to suffer change from without," he wrote in *The Republic*. The human soul, schooled by rational discipline, is released at death into the realm of The One, a place and situation where eternal essences remain unqualified and unchanged in their eternal perfection. While Plato thought he had rationally transcended what he considered the imperfect and restlessly quarrelsome pantheon of the Homeric gods and goddesses, the picture of his perfect divine realm is no less mythical.

Plato's successor, Aristotle, moved closer to modern rationality in two ways. He adopted a non-Platonic empiricism by closely observing realms of concrete phenomena. He also defined ultimate reality or God as Thinking about Thinking. Presumably all reality in his system is based on an abstract structure of thought so perfect that it never changes. It is the center, or Final Cause, toward which all concrete things and processes are attracted and moved by the perfect "Unmoved Mover," the other phrase he used to define the Ultimate Reality. Thus in spite of his pioneering move toward an inductive study of phenomena, his basic world view remained close to Plato's. Like Plato he held that changelessness is a higher order of being than anything subject to change. All reality is governed by an ultimately unchanging order. The human mind, freed from passion and prejudice by careful reasoning, moves as closely as humanity can ever move to the realm of the divine. For Aristotle the examination of concrete details in nature and humanity was for the sake of confirming eternal essences arranged in an ascending hierarchy of degrees of changelessness.

What is the connection between the rationalism of Plato and Aristotle and modern scientific rationality? It must be granted that Aristotle's bias on behalf of deductive reason stands in contrast to the sixteenth- and seventeenth-century origins of science, in which empirical facts were given the chance to alter rather than merely confirm rational principles. But even here, certain elements of the transcendence model of changeless unity remained. Right through the time of Newton and beyond, the Greek image of a single, rationally coordinated universe persisted as the goal of science. Everything is what it is by reason of what caused it to be. There is no room for caprice or chance. As Einstein remarked, "God does not throw dice," meaning, I believe, that all disjunctions in scientific explanation are functions of human ignorance rather than genuine paradoxes.

There is no denying that rationalism, whether Hellenic or modern, is anti-mythical. The caprice of the gods, the darkness of fate, the mysteries of divine judgment, the tragic suffering of human heroes, the strange combinations of order and chaos in all events—all became anathema. The myth of a fulfilled and perfect cosmic order took the place of the darker myths of an earlier time. But in seeking to replace *mythos* with *logos*, we had to posit one overarching myth in place of a whole variety of earlier myths.

This is a blunt way of saying that any transcendence model must be founded on some kind of myth, that is, some kind of story and history that is an object of faith rather than proof. And if such is the case, what we call myth is therefore not to be prejudged as false. We call our own myths true, no matter how false many discarded myths look.

THE JUDAIC TRANSCENDENCE MODEL

The same critical disavowal of myth (even while holding to a normative and dominant myth) seems to have occurred in the other mainstream of Western history, in biblical thought. Against the myths of many gods, the ancient Jews defended their faith in one God. Against the pagan tendency to humanize the deeds of divinity, Yahweh looms as infinitely distant, invisible, mysterious, unanalyzable, and unassailable. Against the claims of rival tribes for their own magic and magical rituals, claims with which the Jews were surrounded, the Bible simplifies the relationship of humanity to Yahweh in terms of obedience to his law and petition for his mercy. Against the tendency to describe God in all-too-human images, the Jews looked upon God as above human standards, as well as above all names. For instance, in the Book of Job, God appears as an infinite power transcending any human concept of justice. And among the Hebrew prophets, God is able and willing to challenge the behavior of those whom he has called his chosen people. Here is a God in controversy with those who depend on him. The covenant between God and the Jews was not presumed to be a magical instrument for compelling divine favor. It was held in faith, and the rewards of its faithful keeping were finally ascribed to God's judgment and mercy, not to human decision.

In short, the Jews' rejection of idolatry and their exaltation of one God bound to humanity not through the subtleties of high reasoning but through the keeping of a covenant of righteousness combined to produce a critical attitude toward the welter of mythology in the pagan world. But obviously the Jews did not escape myth; they advanced it, and from the standpoint of our own worldview, they purified it.

THE CHRISTIAN SYNTHESIS

The blending of Hellenic and biblical mythological themes was possible because of the demythologizing tendencies of each. The Jews believed in the ultimate lordship of one God, in power, and in wisdom. It was not difficult for the Alexandrian church fathers to graft this vast image onto the Hellenic vision of the One. The suffering of persons of faith—epitomized in the homelessness of the Jews, in the Passion of Christ, and in the death of the martyrs—found ready compensation in the Hellenic vision of a pure realm, transcendent over all and the eternal home of all faithful and purified souls. Although this doctrinal system looks mythically complex from our vantage point, it is a common theme from Tertullian through Augustine to Luther, a theme that states that Christian doctrine is extremely simple, direct, and comprehensible, that it is a truth thoroughly cleansed of all the speculations and bizarre imaginations of pagan myth. What classical and biblical culture hold in common is the vision of an orderly and reasonable cosmos and of a rightful and exalted place for humanity in the midst of it.

Upon the firm foundations of this comprehensive transcendence model, modern science was founded. Against the flux of time, science in its early and classical stages sought to find quasi-permanent structures for which it used the metaphor of "the laws of nature." Against the diversity of phenomena, science sought to push its research back to nature's ultimate building blocks, the atoms or uncuttable elements of reality. Against the vagaries of human free will and wandering or unfulfilled human purposes, science sought to construe reality as ordered rather than capricious and determined rather than spontaneous. From this vantage point the anthropomorphisms of the biblical Yahweh look excessively mythical. It is not surprising that biblical theology was made more abstract, impersonal, and qualified in an Aristotelian direction by such diverse thinkers as Maimonides, Aquinas, and Spinoza.

In contemporary science only traces of the Christian transcendence model remain. One must lop off the old Platonic hope for an ecstatic vision of the One. But we keep the image of a coordinated and purposeless system, details of which are available to our partial and never-perfect understanding. We lop off the biblical image of God the Judge and Redeemer, but we keep the notion that in the course of time natural selection "decides" what is capable of survival and what must cease to perpetuate its kind. In a Platonic fashion we argue that the way to acquaintance with and use of the stable orders of the cosmos is the way of rational knowledge, although we lop off the idea of a direct connection between mind and the Ideal and we substitute the necessity to invent and test models drawn from empirical observation. We keep the biblical sense of a linear history, of an evolution in time moving toward higher forms, but we lop off the idea that God foresees and plans this drama in advance. Instead we substitute the idea of random variation and natural selection in place of human purpose and divine judgment. Finally, if we are asked what is the meaning of the whole process as far as human life is concerned, some may give a quasi-Socratic answer—insight; others may give a quasi-biblical answer—survival and well-being; still others may give no answer and avow that none can be found.

The foregoing transcendence model of science has or had mythical elements going back to original Greek and biblical habits of perception and symbolism. Surviving fragments of myth may be noted (1) in the conception of laws of nature, implying the drama of a governing agency promulgating and enforcing its decrees; (2) in the conception of natural selection, implying the drama of a cosmic editing or judging or deciding of relative survival powers; and (3) in the concept of evolution toward a higher, more complex structure of reality, implying the drama of a history moving toward (if not directly to) a grand finale or climax point.

CAN WE AVOID ALL TRANSCENDENCE MODELS?

It is clear that portions of biblical and/or Hellenic myth remain in the modern mind and color its functions. However, just as the Greeks, the Jews, and the Christians, each in their way, tried to purify the myths of previous ages, may all myths be finally expunged from modern religious discourse? Such a process would in effect end forever any doctrine of transcendence. We would cease to say that there is a process indirectly revealed to us through mythological symbols selected from but transcending the phenomenal world. Can this be done?

One would have to give up any image of a stable and orderly reality transcending human consciousness. The only order would be the provisional orders of human behavior and invented by human symbolism. The coordination of symbol and fact would refer to human impulses and responses, no more. History, whether of groups or of individuals, would be stripped of all purpose and progress. In other words, the "meaning" of history would be only fleetingly bestowed on selected moments by individuals. Each moment would thus be freed to mean anything. And each moment would mean different things to different people.

Such a worldview would be so close to chaos that it would be difficult to resist a counteracting intrusion of transcendence models in the form of covert mythical images. Thus we would have to guard against the rise of the image of humanity as a definable entity. Our ethics, law, and custom would need to be constantly defended from *a priori* categorization. We would need to depend for standards of value ultimately upon the impulse of each human agent. The degree to which any such impulse were sufficiently supported and adopted by others to survive even temporarily would have to suffice as a dominant ethical standard. Justice would be measured in terms of survival and conquest. We would have to conclude that what one values is a function of what one wants and what one is enabled and permitted to have by his/her environment. We would have to chase away the remnants of a myth of the soul (which says that one's individuality is sacred or of worth); we would also have to chase away a myth of the neighbor (which claims that what one encourages or prevents in others is only an extension of what one wants for oneself). Altruism would be dead.

Emerson's statement that "man is a myth-bearing tree" is confirmed in the subtle prevalence and persistence, even in this scientific age, of transcendence models containing concrete and dramatic elements. The very rationalism that seeks to substitute a total *logos* for all *mythos* makes its appeal to a hidden transcendence model. In this model, the human brain is given the primary position of judge over the flux of events out of which, as part of a living organism, it arises and operates. It asks for a self-contained transcendence over rival conceptions such as Marxism, Freudianism, behaviorism, etc. The brain presses ever steadily toward the goal of understanding its own process, as though it were really two realities: an objective thinking machine whose operations can be measured and predicted, and a subjective thinker who can make judgments about everything, including the objective thinking machine. The picture of a brain transcending and knowing itself is as subtly mythical as anything found in the Bible or ancient Greece.

It may be objected that any worldview or system of values that remains within the human sphere could hardly be called transcendent, especially in view of the fact that it maintains a modest reserve toward cosmic belief or universal speculation. Nonetheless, although it appears to be more modest than its predecessors, it is actually less so. It says that humanity is the true and sole measurer and author of its own meaning and destiny. Further, it exalts not humanity as a generalized communal entity, but rational, conscious, deliberate, scientific humanity, and it relegates to positions of lesser importance and authority all the other faces and facets of humanity we have come to acknowledge within brief human history.

The devotees of scientific rationalism put their faith ultimately in the conscious human self, in its decisive behavior rather than in its unconscious self, in its reason rather than its instinct, in its observational and analytical skills rather than its artistic and synthetic skills. Finally, and perhaps most important of all, basic trust is lodged in a presupposed harmony of the unity of all rational persons. On the contrary, the society of science is constantly riven by radical disagreement and gives no promise of ever reaching even a unity of method, much less a unity of substance. Such a model thus transcends and strays from human experience by leaving out a huge volume of those who find truth in the arts or religion or both, as well as in science. Of all the transcendence models of our time, one of the least logical, least empirical, least credible is that of autonomous scientific humanity providing successfully, over a long passage of time, for its own well-being.

A TRANSCENDENCE MODEL FOR OUR DAY

Our argument is arriving at two critical considerations. The first is that to deny a transcendence model, one must first bring forward another transcendence model, either consciously or unconsciously. The second is that the particular transcendence model that has largely prevailed for a long time among the intelligentsia of the Western world is in need of radical criticism and renovation. Our choice is not whether we shall commit our allegiance to any transcendence model at all, but which models most nearly reflect the full range of our experience and are therefore most worthy of our loyalty.

The major characteristic feature of the modern experience of reality is its dynamism. Therefore, any credible transcendence model in our day must point to a process rather than to any allegedly eternal or static reality. Even if the new model retains the older abstract principle that the whole universe is one, its unity must be sharply qualified. It will be an associative or societal model of unity, having infinite internal divisions and partial disjunctions. The One may be eternal, but it is not eternally the same. It will be envisaged as having a history with evolving potentialities moving toward fulfillment and with dying actualities moving toward extinction. Nothing is a finished perfection. There are no ultimate building blocks, no invariant and timeless achievements. In developing novelty while remaining ultimately harmonious, this model is value-creating and value-sustaining. Its aim is to endure while changing, to sustain unity while experimenting with new forms. Although it is coordinated with respect to broad limits of possibility, it is highly random and experimental within these limits.

It begins to appear that the larger cosmic processes in which we dwell exhibit features parallel to our own features. Just as we experiment with novelty and wait to see whether it will work—that is, whether this novel action can make sense in coordination with wider ranges of action—so all life has its random experiments, its persistence in new styles, its governance within surrounding ecologies, its judgments of success or failure, life or death. Furthermore, we can push the organismic analogy from the living to the nonliving on the assumption that the adjustment of inorganic environments is both coordinated and random, that such environments contain unrealized potentialities waiting for actualization, one being that life itself emerges from nonlife. Ultimately, life and nonlife in this model are one, not by the degrading of life into something other than itself but rather by the lodging of both the living and the nonliving in a single creative and dynamic matrix.

To proceed in this direction calls up the image of the living God and requires that one use symbols that are in some respects anthropomorphic. The justification for such usage is partly phenomenological; that is, human beings will filter their realizations through essentially human media. This is to acknowledge that the process that produces and sustains life is at least as complex and rich in texture as all forms of life, including ourselves, plus much more of which we know nothing. Beyond ourselves, persons can suppose only an infinite complexity. Thus the images of this transcendence model become more literary and artistic, less Platonic and abstract, more mythic and less abstract.

Once it is considered possible as well as desirable to construe the universe in quasihuman images as well as in impersonal terms, further basic principles emerge, this time in symbols that are more mythical than abstract. The imagery of struggle, triumph, reverse, disaster, and renewal in humanity provides a model for the quasi-historical adventure of all of nature, in part and in the whole. The entire cosmos is cast in the form not of a mechanical system but of a drama in which vast issues are slowly developing and under-going crisis and renewal. A person's or a society's place in this drama is not a matter of indifference; it is portentous with conse-quences for good and for ill. The fact that the details of the drama are partially revealed and partially hidden is no excuse for with-drawal or irresponsibility. Just as the individual in each evolving species plays out its "role" to the utmost in the hope and faith that its individual vigor and persistence make sense in the overall sur-vival picture, so each person in his/her more complex role strug-gles both in darkness and in faith. Human consciousness being much broader than animal consciousness, our role is correspond-ingly more complex than animal roles. Where the instincts of animals, derived from their genetic structure, are the final deter-minants of their success or failure to adapt and survive, human beings must depend upon observation, reason, and cultural pat-tern, as well as biological instinct. Our opportunities and prob-lems of adaptation are both broader and more difficult.

If, as it is supposed, there are life-forms in other planets that are different from and possibly more complex than any on this planet, then their opportunities and adaptations will be corre-spondingly broader and more complex. To the denizens of some superior planet, our anthropomorphisms would appear inade-quate in relation to the complexity of reality as they feel it. Their "religions," if any, would aim at imputing no less than the highest qualities of their own experience to their model of the Whole.

The religious use of a transcendence model is not for the sake of giving the believer a weapon with which to coerce fellow be-lievers, contrary believers, or nonbelievers. Quite the contrary, the aim of this model is to induce such a respect for the Whole and for oneself as part of the Whole that one's response to life is both vital and tolerant, both reverential and critical, rather than careless, condescending, and coercive. Within such a framework science becomes a major cultural tool and, in company with art and the humanities, a major means for expressing the glory of phenomena and of respecting the orders by which all earthly phenomena—including humanity—may fruitfully coexist.

It is more logical to trust the process out of which we come, in spite of its vagaries, mischances, and misjudgments of individuals or groups, than to trust humanity exclusively, all the while alleging neutrality or even hostility to the very primordial processes that brought humanity into being. Since the part cannot be separated from the whole, the part cannot be loved or trusted separately. An exclusive religious humanism is essentially irrational and humanism in a theistic setting makes much more sense. That is, the transcendence model that adequately supports any basic faith in the human venture must include more than the human venture per se.

A major problem in the credibility of this kind of transcendence model is the persistent mind-set in our day toward keeping a clear disjunction between the organic and inorganic. How can we move from a sense for an impersonal machine-like system to a living evolving history? The appeal I would make, beyond what has already been said about everyday human experience and its logic, is the experience of ecstasy. When one is grasped by an intense impression of value, whether concentrated in a sharply defined object or more generally diffused over the environment, one has the choice either of suppressing all response, thereby denying one's own experience, or of looking for means to celebrate communally and objectively the high voltage of the value impact one has undergone. The modern age tends to play it cool, attributing all deep enthusiasm or agony to the perceiver rather than to the perceived. The transcendence model I am espousing does the opposite. It does not limit love or hate, union or disjunction to the subjective pole of experience. It expresses and understands these hot interactions as real interactions, and it counts as honorable the poet or priest who gives voice to such intensity by metaphor and anthropomorphic image.

Obviously there is something childlike in this kind of symbolic response to life. Furthermore, children do not always distinguish between reality and neurosis; many of their intense reactions are largely internal and objectively unfounded. Therefore, the mature person who remains childlike must also be more than childlike. He/she must develop critical intelligence and strive to distinguish between inner and outer realities. In the maturity of any culture, the sciences develop for the same reason. There is no question that our civilization needs this kind of intellectual acumen. But equally important for civilization is the quality of passionate love not only of other persons but also of the environment that is our life support. Such human caring in the religious mode is a sense of the sacred. I think it is possible to be simultaneously childlike and mature, worshipful and scientific.

These arguments in favor of enlarging the transcendence model of our thinking are not designed to conflict with scientific rationalism but rather to broaden the bases of its operation. I put no artificial boundary upon any kind of scientific procedure, no matter how its conclusions threaten the literal meanings of mythical stories. The prospect of remythologizing is designed to keep up with the more complex picture of reality the sciences are developing. The world of science and religion as seen in the eighteenth and nineteenth centuries is already overpassed. Let us hope that science and religion may develop in mutually tolerant and supportive ways in the new world that is upon us.

A New Story of Creation

Most people at all knowledgeable about the sciences today believe that evolution theory is the closest we can come to knowing how the great diversity of life on our planet developed. I am confident that evolutionism has triumphed, should triumph, and will continue to triumph over any and every attempt to make biblical creationism a substitute for science. And yet I do not wish to discard the biblical creation stories of Genesis 1 and 2 as irrelevant simply because I do not believe them to be factually true. Why should we let the fundamentalist interpretations of the Bible triumph? Biblical literalism is the surest way of destroying the dignity, the majesty, and the wisdom of biblical literature.

In the prescientific ages when these stories were told and later written, I have no doubt that their people believed them literally. In those days there was little or no distinction between mythology and history or science and art. We rightly make such distinctions. In so doing, we increase our appreciation of the Bible's fine literary art. Do we refuse to read or see *Hamlet* because one of the characters is a ghost or *Macbeth* because three of the characters are supernatural witches? I claim that we can profit by the biblical symbolism in Genesis even if we do not we believe in the story literally, even if we do not believe in God.

Let me begin with a few words about the curious existence of two creation stories side by side in the first two chapters of the Bible. The second creation story found in Genesis 2:4 and following is attributed to an earlier source called J (for Yahweh), which is pre-exilic, that is, written before the Babylonians conquered Israel in 586 BCE. Chapter 1 is from a later post-exilic source called P (that is, Priestly). I suspect but cannot prove that the first chapter of Genesis, the Priestly version, is an attempt to purify the second chapter, even though chapter 2 is the more traditional, that is, more materialistic, describing Adam's creation, as well as that of other animals, from the dust of the ground and Eve's from Adam's body. P has creation occurring more mystically and non-materially, as an instantaneous response to divine speech: God says thus and so, and lo, it comes to be. Nevertheless, the two chapters are complementary.

Human beings have always tended to distinguish themselves from their mammalian forebears on the basis of our ability to turn reality into symbols and to invent new realities by means of symbols, especially language and mathematics. *Homo sapiens* is the one kind of animal we know that uses words, numbers, and language and ultimately depends on these devices for survival. It is not surprising, then, that Genesis 1 has God creating by means of the divine voice, by the use of words. This is a principal instance of God being created in the image of humanity.

My first reason for appreciating Genesis 1 is precisely its mysterious flavor. It anticipates our contemporary fascination with the mystery of creativity. *Creativity* is the great buzzword today, not only for the arts, but for education, for economic enterprise, for science, for glorifying just about everything that looks good to us, including the crayon drawings done by little children. We are fascinated by the way ingenious people create more out of less. Our educational and scholarly traditions make much of the mystery of creativity. By definition real human creativity, whether in the arts or sciences, requires an element of spontaneity for which there is no rule or formula, something transcending the merely predictable. The Genesis 1 creation story celebrates creativity as the appearance of more from less in the whole interdependent web of existence. Genesis 1 is a poetic glorification of an expanding universe in the metaphor of divine artistry. And any metaphor can be true without being literal fact. Genesis 1 preserves a sense of mysterious wonder.

Does the sentence in Genesis 1 "God saw that it was good" really mean "God saw to it that it would be good" or "God found it to be good" after the experimental deed? If the former alternative is accepted, it means that the Creator knew there would be success in creating a divinely perfect creation. However, the past tense "God saw that it was good" suggests there was no such foresight. It looks much more like divine surprise. In the official Hebrew-to-English translation made by the Jewish Publication Society of America in 1962, they say their concern is to clear up questions raised by inaccuracies in the King James translation. In their English text we have "God saw how good the light was," using the same words throughout the chapter with each creative episode. Then comes a change in verse 31, "God saw all that he had made, and found it very good." How can we get divine omniscience out of that?

My second reason for appreciating the Genesis creation stories is this subtle suggestion of experiment, improvisation, and divine surprise in chapter 1. Although the older, second chapter lacks the lyrical symmetry of Genesis 1 and is confusing as to how much was thought to have existed before the Divine started to work on it, what appeals to me about this cruder tale is that it is even more improvisational than its later version in the Priestly source. In Genesis 2 God first makes an earth and a heaven. Nothing grows on the earth because of lack of rain, and even if something could grow, there is no one to till the ground. Fortunately, in the fashion of the ancient Near Eastern desert, springs of water flow mysteriously up from the ground, and evidently plant life is stimulated by this water as one might expect. In this version plants do not come by divine fiat. God's primary concern then is to create some kind of creature to farm this wild growth and presumably have that creature subsist on its vegetarian diet. So God breathes into a handful of dust and out comes Adam, first of all fauna to be found among the manifold flora. In this respect Genesis differs radically from our evolution theory, which puts *Homo sapiens* at the end of a long string of evolved fauna. Then, improvising step by step, God's next improvement is to establish a garden for Adam to care for and enjoy. Among all the delightful plants in the garden is a mysterious tree of the knowledge of good and evil. Adam is free to eat any of the garden's produce except the fruit of that one tree. To eat that forbidden fruit will be the death of him. Why this strange command? You would think that the deity who later spends most of human-related history insisting on human righteousness would want the firstborn son to know right from wrong at the very beginning. Is God jealous lest the man whom God has put in charge of the world, whom the Divine later commissions to name all the other species to appear around him, will use the power of speech and other arts and technologies to pollute and destroy the earth? Perhaps so. In any case, given global warming we still need to work on the problems of right from wrong.

At any rate, God finds another weakness in the divine work, saying, "It is not good that the man should be alone. I will make him a helper as his partner." Again we hear of a new improvisational quasi-evolutionary episode. How different that seemingly small detail is from Genesis 1, in which everything the Creator does and everywhere the Creator looks he sees nothing but good. And what does God do to provide Adam with a helper and partner? God rushs ahead to create a vast population of fauna and brings them to Adam to name them and to see if they can help him. Is God hoping that at least one of these species, possibly the dog or the cat or the horse, would prove to be adequate helpers and partners? Nobody can call that kind of blind experimentation omniscience. This is a case of divine stupidity. The Bible frankly admits that God has many failures in this helpmate project: "...for the man there was not found a helper for his partner." Thereupon God has to change tactics: In a magnificent burst of creativity, God performs the only open-heart caesarian ever achieved before or since, and out came Eve, a woman. Adam may be innocent of good and evil, but he certainly knows the difference between a beautiful young woman and every other kind of animal, for he shouts immediately, "This is at last bone of my bones and flesh of my flesh."

I like that phrase, "at last," as though Adam were informing the Great Improviser that things had finally come out right. The biblical writer then comments:

> Therefore a man leaves his father and his mother and clings to his wife and they become one flesh. And the man and his wife were both naked and were not ashamed.

Unlike the early Christian suspicions about sex, Genesis uses the lovely phrase "they become one flesh," adding with considerable frankness, "the man and his wife were both naked and were not ashamed."

I am fascinated by the image of the great God who, in the first chapter of Genesis, names light and darkness, earth and sea, and sun, moon, and stars, then does not name a single biological species. God gives that job to Adam and must know that the power of naming, the power of the word, is analogous to just one of God's own powers: creating by linguistic means. This image of God delegating the naming function to humanity is quite modern: It tallies with the notion that human understanding is a human invention, not something handed down in Platonic essences or in mystical visions or literal revelations.

I find support for this trial-and-error approach to creation from another nonscientific source, a quotation I gleaned from a

book describing that great body of ancient Jewish biblical commentary, the Talmud:

> Twenty-six attempts preceded the present genesis, all of which
> were destined to fail. The world of man has arisen out of the
> chaotic heart of preceding debris; he too is exposed to the risk
> of failure, and the return to nothing. "Let's hope it works this
> time" said God as he created the world, and this hope, which
> has accompanied all the subsequent history of the world and
> humanity, has emphasized right from the outset that this his-
> tory is branded with the mark of radical uncertainty.

Humanity was created "out of the heart of preceding debris"—
is that a picture of a "very good" world, much less the production
of a perfect and all-powerful Creator? Even as I like the poetic ex-
pressiveness of Genesis 1, I like even more the improvisational nature of divine creativity, in contrast to the usual assumption of
divine omniscience and omnipotence. It is more nearly evolutionary in spite of its great compression of time frame. This poetic
metaphor tallies nicely with the gradual nature of evolution, the
slow development of living forms by means of chance mutations
and unforeseen adaptations.

Nevertheless, I have another stronger reason for treasuring both
of the first two chapters of Genesis. But before I say what it is, let us
take a brief look at chapter 3, the story of the so-called Fall of Man.
I depart radically from the usual understanding of it. It is not a fall;
it is a rise, a rise of persons to full humanity. Eve has the courage to
eat the apple and serve it to Adam, such that they both become truly
human, not simply innocent gardeners. God may have the wisdom
to know goodness in and of itself apart from evil. But humanity can
understand neither good nor evil without the reality and contrast of
each with the other. Human life became infinitely richer, more complex and problematic than Eden's mere bowl of cherries. Without
deprecating in any way the joys of gardening, the thought that this
would be the limit of human endeavor for all eternity suggests a vast
boredom. Three cheers for Eve's defiance!

God does not destroy God's children because of their mature disobedience. They are sent forth, clothed literally for bodily protection and metaphorically to face all the ambiguities of the actual system of existence, where natural order mingles with chance and random choice, where finite persons are free to rebel against any established order, where good and evil are present and felt. I doubt that Werner Heisenberg got his uncertainty principle from the Bible, but it is surprisingly close to what is anticipated there.

This is the great paradox of all existence, not simply of humanity. Creation may have looked good to God in the beginning, but from my perspective God learned that mere goodness is not enough. There has to be change, and with change, the risk of evil. The primary paradox of the goodness of reality is that it is also subject to destruction. From this inherent paradox, a number of more specialized paradoxes emerge, such as life is beautiful versus life is unfair, and the world is good versus the world is inexorably fatal to all living things, and it is wonderful to be alive versus life can be so terrible as to cause one to wish for death.

Furthermore, the negative side of each statement of paradox can easily become dominant. We ask petulantly, why should anything good have to die or even suffer? Why does evil persist no matter how much good we hope for and work for? Why do we, who think we are good, sometimes create evil? Why, according to the second law of thermodynamics, will everything we know of the wonders of existence eventually burn out to nothingness? Even the atoms will perish. Every species ever born, all that is of earth will one day be absorbed into the life-giving sun's red giant-hood. Surely these overwhelming paradoxes cannot be traced merely to the disobedience of poor little Adam and Eve.

I hold that the only way to live with a true paradox is to have the courage to recognize both sides of it, not to exaggerate the positive side or ignore or deny the side that one fears or abhors. Genesis 1 emphasizes the positive side; Genesis 2 introduces an ominous foretaste of the negative side. Genesis 3 faces up to the negative/positive aspect of our human existence. It takes all three chapters to show in poetic and metaphorical language the full human condition. In short, my third and fullest reason to appreciate Genesis 1 and 2 is the manner in which Genesis 3 completes an otherwise incomplete picture of human existence.

The glorious, full-orchestral refrain "And God saw that it was good," even "very good," is there to remind us that goodness is as immortal as reality, that hope is never out of season no matter how many must fall under the burden of despair. It is there to remind us that we are not alone, that the stars will come on at night without our pushing a button, that the best things in life are more often gifts from beyond, rather than human achievements.

I count Genesis 1 and 2 as a hallelujah chorus of blessing upon all of reality out of which evolved the gift of human life. The final verses in Genesis 1 coming right after the last creation, that of Adam and Eve, are these:

> God blessed them and God said to them, "Be fruitful and multiply and fill the earth and subdue it; and have dominion over the fish of the sea and over the birds of the air and over every living thing that moves upon the earth."

So translates the New Revised Standard Version. But in the King James version, the verb *fill* in "fill the earth" is translated *replenish*. "Be fruitful and multiply and replenish the earth and subdue it."

In biblical times there was no problem of overpopulation, overconsumption, or pollution of the good resources of the earth. There was no need for balancing human greed with a self-sustaining ecology. Probably *fill* and *replenish* are synonymous in the Hebrew, but thanks to the Elizabethan translators, who may have worked better than they knew, we are admonished to replenish all that we spoil.

Thus, my major reason for respecting the wisdom of Genesis 1 and 2 is God's enthusiasm for creation. Despite death and all human suffering, these stories strike me as an ultimate blessing of all reality, not a neutral cosmology.

What is a blessing? Blessing is a sense of worth or benefit derived from beyond one's own conscious will or contrivance, a kind of gift from the outside to one's inner strength and felicity. Specifically, God blesses Adam and Eve by giving them enormous power over all that is. I think that that sense of gift has to be acknowledged regardless of our theological outlook, requiring that our uses and manipulations of nature be sustainable, not predatory. We are given far more than we receive or are ever able to achieve. When humanity's pride, its needs and greed, transcend and obscure the sacredness of all on which we depend, we are in deep trouble.

It is in this spirit that William James was fascinated by the writings of the nineteenth-century German scientist Gustav Fechner. Fechner saw the earth as a huge and nourishing organism, much vaster than any one or all of its many species, much wiser than we are in the ways in which it balances its conflicts. Even our driest deserts, the long reaches of empty sea, and our spherical canopy of air have their ecological roles, which are among the very blessings upon which our existence depends. In a time when belief in angels was common, Fechner scolded those who thought of angels as pure spirit eternally existent. He believed in matter. He saw the earth as our true guardian angel, and if we need further angelic help, we might look to the other heavenly bodies, mainly the sun, not to thin bodiless spirits.

This kind of outlook demands the most care from those who have the most power in the whole ecological family. We who are so richly blessed have least excuse for exploiting and damaging the very gifts by which our lives and many other kinds of life are possible.

It appears to me that liberal religious sentiment is gradually moving away from the position that worth, values, sacredness are vested only in the human species and that all else is mere stuff, devoid of worth except as we can experiment with it, use it, and exploit it. We are beginning to rediscover the concept that the nonhuman worlds are sacred in their own right. We are beginning to sympathize with the Native Americans who regard earth and sky as their primary relatives, the interdependent web of their being, and the receivers of their sacrifices and deaths. As a church, we are aiming to rediscover and practice ways of thanksgiving not just for our lives as human beings, not just for plant and animal life, but for all the richness of all reality, inorganic as well as organic, upon which we depend.

Many years ago it was my good fortune to be at a conference with Harlow Shapley, a then-famous astronomer on the Harvard faculty. I remember his imagining a meeting between himself and Albert Schweitzer. Shapley said, "I would say to him, 'Al, you have done a good job promoting the idea of 'Reverence for Life.' But you need to go one step further: you need to say, 'Reverence for Being.'"

The Greek Hero and the
Biblical Anti-hero

WHETHER WE REGARD THEM as literal accounts, fiction, or something in between, certain ancient stories have a decided formative effect on both religious institutions and the larger culture. We often define our values by these stories—not only by their events but by the particular artistic expressions in which they are handed down to us. Narrative style, characterization, and creative choices all influence the values transmitted by our sacred mythologies. In his book *Mimesis*, Erich Auerbach compares the literary style of Homer with that of the biblical Elohist writer, especially with regard to episodes in Homer's *Odyssey* and the twenty-second chapter of Genesis.

The *Odyssey* story comes to a tense moment when Odysseus, having returned to his palace in disguise, almost loses the advantage of secrecy and anonymity when his old nurse recognizes a familiar scar on his ankle while she is bathing his feet. We watch the hero grasp the old woman by the throat to prevent her outcry, while the divine protectress Athena diverts wife Penelope's attention from the scene. At this dramatic moment Homer interrupts his story in a flashback of some seventy lines, telling in a vivid and leisurely fashion the precise details of Odysseus' youthful boar hunt from which the scar derived. The author is not holding his reader in suspense. He is simply shifting the ground of his narrative to a different time and place. And he just as easily shifts back to Odysseus and the nurse when the earlier event is fully narrated. Auerbach uses this and other examples of Homeric storytelling to assert that even in the earliest centuries of Greek literature, the writers are concerned to give a three-dimensional picture of the principal characters. The lineage and history of individuals, an account of their accomplishments and skills, their crimes and achievements, and above all, the outcome of their destiny are the foci of every story. Whether the gods favored or opposed them is important only as contributing to the events of their human career. If the story is a god story, it is treated in the same human and heroic narrative style.

How different is Genesis 22 when an undescribed God speaks to an unlocated man and commands the sacrifice of that man's only direct heir and beloved son, Isaac. Nothing of Abraham's "moment" on Mount Moriah—whether his physical situation or his inner feeling—is stated directly. The story concentrates exclusively on God's right and power to command and later prevent this horrendous deed and on Abraham's unquestioning, even hurried obedience. Most of Genesis 22 is an implied background, the infinite deeps of God's majesty and of Abraham's faith and woe.

Auerbach's principal method of comparison is literary. He points to the vastly contrasting style of the two authors: the Greek endlessly wordy, logical, precise; the Hebrew laconic, existentially portentous, and vague. Each of the two literary styles corresponds to one of two lifestyles and transcendence models, contrasting standards as to what it means to be fully human. Odysseus is known by his deeds, skills, accomplishments, and ingenuity, as in the way he masters the dangers of the youthful boar hunt and in the way he slays the hoard of suitors pursuing his wife and house during his absence in the Trojan War. He is what the Greeks called a hero, and the Western world has adopted the word *hero* as the principal name of any literary protagonist.

By contrast to the image of the heroic, Abraham, the father of the people of the covenant, is not known for his powers, skill, or cunning; he has no prowess in warfare, statecraft, or rhetoric, no poetry of utterance that his words might become immortal. His fame is probably more widespread and potentially more enduring than that of Odysseus. But for what? For his belief that he was chosen by the Creator of heaven and earth to be the father of a holy people and commanded to journey from his homeland in the lower Mesopotamian valley to the distant land of what is now Israel. He responds to this unsolicited divine initiative in his life with absolute trust and obedience despite his human frailty. He is old, undistinguished in wealth and power, suspect of partial infertility, subject to the jealous command of his wife in exiling his son born to a concubine, supine and submissive before Pharaoh's desire to steal his wife. He is a simple desert nomad and shepherd. There is nothing of the Greek hero in Abraham. Why should his descendants remember him? Or how is it that his name should be inscribed for righteousness for more than two and a half millennia of his children's children? Odysseus today is a familiar character in an ancient and eloquent fable; Abraham is an enduring exemplar. The one, a man of many wiles, shares his wisdom, as Alfred North Whitehead remarked, with the foxes; the other is the patriarch of Judaism, Christianity, and Islam.

If the contrast in ideal type between Odysseus and Abraham seems too absolute to admit comparison, let us turn to two figures more nearly alike: the military heroes Achilles and David. At the beginning of Homer's *Iliad*, consider what happens when Achilles' commander-in-chief, Agamemnon, steals from Achilles the Trojan maid Briseus, Achilles' prize of war. The wrath of Achilles against his commander becomes the first word in the epic and the focal point for a vast drama of gods and men that determines not only the ultimate tragedy of the defeat of Troy, but all the suffering of Greeks and Trojans and the final death of Achilles by a treacherous shot of a poisoned arrow. One could argue that the *Iliad* is a mighty drama founded on relatively simple, basic human drives and emotions, all of which are clearly and unambiguously described. Homer's epic style, as Auerbach says, has no background.

In the twenty-third chapter of 2 Samuel, we have a little legend from the Philistine campaigns of David (perhaps the nearest biblical equivalent of the Greek "hero") when "three mighty men" slip through the Philistine lines and, at great risk of their lives, bring to King David not a woman but a little fresh water from the well by the gate of his boyhood home, Bethlehem. In four verses the Bible narrative is completed: David, recognizing the courage of his benefactors, will not give himself the pleasure of drinking their offering of water. Instead he likens it to the blood of the three valiant soldiers and pours it out into the dry soil as an offering to God. In this story David is the recipient of an unsolicited gift, and he returns the gift to his God, completing a circle of generosity like the covenant itself. David's act is symbolic of a kind of divine-human symbiosis, a vast drama in which men figure in many layers and levels of involvement toward a triumphant divine-human climax. The world of Achilles is a world of competing powers, both human and divine, a world in which prerogatives are arbitrarily established by brute power and then jealously guarded by the sword, or by law, or by rhetoric to the farthest reaches of tragic outcome. Achilles' world is one in which conflict is endemic and tragedy unavoidable. His heroism consists in his disciplined power and skill to create, manage, and endure a dangerous life, and finally to die with his honor intact. Even his dependency upon the help of certain gods, including his divine mother, Thetis, is a means, a tool for coping with life's savagery before the inevitable onslaught of "dusty death." David's world, although as replete with hazard and suffering as Achilles', is built upon the rock of a divinely ordained and humanly accepted covenant, a world established in the form of a divine comedy. Religion is not a tool to enlist the support of the gods; it is a joyful acknowledgment of the supreme power of God's irresistible judgment and ultimate benevolence, in short, God's ultimate fruitful sovereignty over history. Abraham's transcendence model is built upon the image of an all-powerful Creator God; Homer's, upon the hazard of personal strength and courage and the ability to enlist the help of a friendly divine agent against a hostile one.

For generations the imagination of the Western mind has been fascinated by its Greek and its biblical prototypes. In their professions of faith, the overwhelming majority of Europeans and Americans have leaned toward the biblical pattern. But in style of action and standards of character, the Greek model seems to dominate Western culture. We live in a world of constant economic and political competition. And especially in America, success and power are more fundamentally honored than righteousness or obedience to divine destiny. Tertullian was sure that Jerusalem should have nothing to do with Athens. But this radical barrier in the inner space of Western humanity is hopelessly broken down. All of us are Greeks and Jews by cultural inheritance. And therein lies the creativity and malaise of Western civilization. We could not be as we are without our twofold heritage. And yet I see no possibility of lasting compatibility, much less real synthesis between the hero and the anti-hero. They will not mix except in uneasy juxtaposition within our cultures, our cities, our minds, and our own skins.

THE CHOICE OF ACHILLES

One may focus the Greek concept of the hero through a fateful incident in Book 9 of Homer's *Iliad*. Agamemnon, chief of the Greek army besieging Troy, being hard-pressed by Achilles' wrathful refusal to commit himself or his men to the Greeks' losing battles, tries to make peace with Achilles. He sends a generous offer of restitution to Achilles via a deputation headed by the wily and thoroughly political Odysseus. After discreetly tempting Achilles with Agamemnon's lavish gifts, Odysseus seeks to put the matter on a high and rational plane, urging him to bottle up "the anger of the proud heart, for consideration is better." Achilles' answer is one of tragic simplicity: He says that he has labored for Agamemnon, and the commander has dishonored him by the theft of the maiden Briseis. He observes that other men besides Agamemnon love their women. He avows that he will quietly get into his ship on the morrow and take himself and his men home. Then follows one of the most revealing passages in the entire epic: A moment of truth comes to Achilles concerning the meaning of the Trojan War. In the Richard Lattimore translation, Achilles says

> Of possessions,
> Cattle and fat sheep are things to be had for the lifting,
> and tripods can be won, and the tawny high heads of horses,
> But a man's life cannot come back again, it cannot be lifted,
> Nor captured again by force, once it has crossed the teeth's barrier.

Here Achilles says quite plainly that the pillage of the Trojan countryside (in addition to the capture of Troy and the rescue of Helen) is a major reason for the war. These warriors are fighting primarily to steal. And Achilles questions whether such agony and its daily risk of death are worth the effort. The reader may think at this point that a simple hedonism is being raised above the classic transcendence model of military honor and eternal fame. But not necessarily. Achilles continues:

> For my mother Thetis, the goddess of the silver feet, tells me
> I carry two sorts of destiny toward the day of my death. Either,
> If I stay here and fight beside the city of the Trojans,
> My return home is gone, but my glory shall be everlasting;
> But if I return home to the beloved land of my fathers,
> The excellence of my glory is gone, but there will be a long life
> Left for me, and my end in death will not come to me quickly.
> And this would be my counsel to others also, to sail back
> Home again, since no longer shall you find any term set
> On the sheer city of Ilion, since Zeus of the wide brows has strongly
> Held his own hand over it, and its people are made bold.

Achilles has neatly described the human ideal and transcendence model of the seasoned hero. He argues that men go to war partly for pillage, partly for honor. If they survive the gaining of pillage, they can take it home and enjoy it along with fame and honor. But if they press forward in war to higher levels of honor, they risk an early death and the loss of their pillaged wealth. Their only compensation, not theirs to enjoy after death, is everlasting fame. More particularly, Achilles argues, at least at this point, that since Zeus appears to have made Troy impregnable, he will sacrifice the chance to augment the treasure of his wealth and his honor. He will go home.

After this episode, Homer shifts his attention to heroes other than Achilles. In a typically detailed account of the gory fortunes of battle, he describes through the next five books the steady advance of the Trojans as they drive the Greeks back to the sea and to their very ships. There is not one mention of Achilles, and the reader might presume—except that Homer would never omit the detail— that Achilles and his Myrmidons have long since departed by sea. But as the Trojans approach the ships, we suddenly meet Patroclus, Achilles' young comrade-in-arms, in great distress telling Achilles of the Greek reverses. Something has kept Achilles from carrying out his original resolution to forsake the land of Troy. When finally in Book 16 the fight moves to the very shadow of the ships, Achilles consents to lend Patroclus his armor and his men. The young Patroclus leaps forth into battle, turns the tide by driving back the enemy, and is ultimately slain by the chief Trojan hero, Hector. The rest is familiar legend. The great personal tragedy of Patroclus' death rouses Achilles to battle. In a complete reversal of his earlier choice, he rushes into war, and after slaughtering the sons of King Priam of Troy, he causes the ignominious death and spoliation of the Trojan hero, Hector. In other classical sources we read of the fall of Troy and the death of Achilles in Troy by treachery.

Driven more by the insult of the tragic death of Patroclus than by his chagrin at the theft of Briseis, Achilles goes to war to avenge his shattered honor. He fulfills the first half of his mother's prophecy and dies young, in everlasting fame, for honor's sake. Honor stands revealed as the real and final dynamic of Achilles' actions. Because of his wounded honor, he at first refuses to fight and for a brief moment sees, in general, the futility of fighting under any circumstances. Because of his lacerated honor at Patroclus' death, he returns to vengeful battle and to his own ultimate tragedy. His ego is the dominant motive force. And in a world of endlessly clashing egos, both human and divine, many other heroes who stand up for themselves and their honor go down to death still young, before the overwhelming odds of the fortunes of war.

The choice of Achilles for honor is a major perspective for interpreting the greater part of Greek hero tales. Jason and the Argonauts risk life repeatedly for the glory of winning the golden fleece and the beautiful Medea. But when Jason turns willfully away from his bride, her revenge is terrible: She murders their children and Jason's new wife. The succession of kings in the House of Atreus lived under a curse in which each felt obliged to avenge his honor against previous murderers. Each king down to Agamemnon himself, including his queen, Clytemnestra, dies violently under the curse of having to avenge their wounded honor. Perhaps the most honorable (in the modern sense) of all the Greek heroes is Oedipus, who, with the best of intentions but not without pride in his political skill and ability to outwit the Delphic oracle, seeks to relieve his city of plague, only to discover that his own crimes are the cause of the plague. He pays the price by blinding himself. But when his sons exile him from the city, he has the self-justifying pleasure of prophesying that they will destroy each other in the wars of succession, as indeed they do. As one reads Sophocles' *Antigone*, one cannot help but be glad that the revenged Oedipus did not live to see his daughter's cruel death in her futile attempt to defend the honor of her fallen brother.

This heroic model is not confined to military prowess alone. The courage to seize and maintain political supremacy in order to defend personal rights is equally important. And for the sake of personal or political power, two additional weapons are important for the figure of the hero: the power of rhetoric and the favor of the gods. The single-minded hero's personal desires have to be universalized in the public eye by rhetorical skill. The hero is an advocate, a debater, an orator, who by eloquence and verbal manipulation can persuade others to his cause and make a public case for the divine righteousness of his own desires. In Homer and in the tragedies, the heroes speak long and eloquently, with the use of many past precedents as though they are arguing their case before the twin courts of human right and divine justice. It is part of the nature of Greek tragedy that antagonists are able to muster equally powerful arguments. What purports to be the civilizing mode of rational persuasion actually intensifies hostility instead of relieving it. All three of the great Athenian tragedians frequently compress the conflicting rhetoric of opponents to one-line antiphonal challenges. One side of a case is presented in one short sentence; the counterargument in the next sentence, and so on, back and forth, through fifteen or twenty lines, each like sword thrusts.

Far more efficacious for the hero than the power of weaponry or rhetoric is the favor of one or more of the gods. We learn in the first book of the *Iliad* that Achilles, while refusing to fight, is content not to make a warlike rebellion against Agamemnon only because he is assured that the goddesses Athena and Hera are his advocates in Olympus. At every fateful point in the battle when some reasonable resolution of the war might occur, either the heroes insist on fighting to preserve their honor or the rivalrous gods, some favoring Greeks and others Trojans, keep the fires of war burning. In Book 4 when the Greeks and Trojans agree to settle their differences by having Paris and Menelaus fight for Helen in personal combat and it appears likely that Paris is going to lose, the truce is broken by the rivalry of the goddesses Athena and

Hera against Aphrodite. In Book 6 when Hector's wife begs him to fight a defensive war from within the walls of the city, he asserts that the city is doomed and argues that the only good he can get from the tragedy is to risk his life in the preservation of his honor. When in Book 14 it appears to the goddess Hera that Zeus has favored the Trojans too drastically, in order to tip the balance of battle toward the Greeks, she distracts Zeus's attention from battle by seducing him, while Poseidon hurries down to the plain of Troy to shore up the weakening Greek defenses. It is by the secret treachery of Apollo that Patroclus is slain in Book 16. In the opening lines of Book 20, Zeus calls the gods into council and bids each of them descend to the battlefield to give aid on whichever side of the battle they choose, while in Olympian grandeur he will remain "upon the fold of Olympus, sitting still, watching, to pleasure my heart." In the climax of the fight between Achilles and Hector, Zeus weighs the soul of each man and decrees Hector's death.

There appears to be an uneasy balance of power among the Olympian gods. Although Zeus is supreme, he may be influenced now this way, now that, by entreaty and persuasion, even by the threats and recalcitrance of the other members of the pantheon. All the agonies of Odysseus and the final success of his long journey home to Ithaca are the reflections of the political wrangling of the divine Poseidon and Athena in rivalry for the favor of Zeus. The brutality of these divine politics is nowhere more blatant than in Book 13 of the *Odyssey* when Poseidon, having failed to prevent the return of Odysseus, is allowed by Zeus to assuage his anger and restore his honor by destroying the peaceful and kindly Phaeacian sailors who had taken Odysseus home. Zeus cannot afford to abide the continuing anger of his powerful brother, Poseidon; this political consideration completely disregards the innocence of the Phaeacian victims.

In point of fact, we cannot read our Judeo-Christian sense of divine justice into the courts of Olympus. The gods are molded into the same concern for their honor and prerogatives as the human heroes are. As Hesiod narrates in his *Theogany*, the gods establish their authority among one another initially by warfare, then by rhetoric and political compromise. The powers of Olympus are evolutionary and divided, founded not upon a code of justice but upon the compensations and expediencies one sees in the continual conflicts of the natural and human world.

The *Theogany* portrays the creation of the world as a series of sexual procreations, followed by the rivalry and warfare of successive generations of divine beings, until Zeus establishes a fragile and uneasy order in the conflict-ridden cosmos. The principal rule, if there is any absolute order, is the rule of compensation. Whatever rises too high must be brought down; whatever causes offense must be avenged; whatever invades prerogatives must be checked and punished. Herein lies the mythological root of Greek pessimism, the melancholy sense of the eternal warfare of existence within itself, of which the inevitable tragedy of the human experience is only one expression. Nature herself is founded in conflict, proceeds and evolves through conflict, and in conflict brings all things to account for the privilege of existence by subsequently subjecting them to the sentence of death. Anaximander's famous dictum (as translated by Martin Nielsen) sums up this general principle: "It is the law of necessity that things should perish and go back to their origin. For they give satisfaction and pay the penalty to one another for their injustice according to the ordinance of time." Apparently Anaximander regarded any form of actual existence itself as a usurpation of the place and station that other potential forms of existence might have occupied but did not. These potential things must be "given justice" by exacting the penalty of death from whatever actually exists. In colloquial language, to exist is to usurp, and the present must move over and make way for a contrasting future.

Perhaps the most eloquent expositor of this tragic-heroic image of existence is the figure of Callicles in his disputes with Socrates in

Plato's *Gorgias*. Listen to Callicles' challenge to the harmonistic rationalism of Socrates (in Benjamin Jowett's translation):

> Nature herself intimates that it is just for the better to have more than the worse, the more powerful than the weaker; and in many ways she shows, among men as well as among animals, and indeed among whole cities and races, that justice consists in the superior ruling over and having more than the inferior.

In an uncanny anticipation of Nietzsche's condemnation of Christianity as a "slave morality," Callicles attacks the moderation and reasonableness of Socrates on the same grounds as Nietzsche would, saying:

> The many... blame the strong man because they are ashamed of their own weakness, which they desire to conceal... And being unable to satisfy their pleasures they praise temperance and justice out of their own cowardice.

The long argument between Socrates and Callicles in the last half of the *Gorgias* exemplifies the struggle among the Greeks for the humanization of the tragic-heroic ideal type. Callicles states in didactic language the ideal human type of the hero that Homer and the tragedians glorified and honored. Socrates tries to turn the image of the hero away from the ethic of conflict to the heroism of the harmonizing intellect devoted to building a rational world of justice and peace. Nowhere is Socrates' mission more compactly stated than in a long speech in the *Gorgias*, directed against Callicles:

> Philosophers tell us, Callicles, that communion and friendship and orderliness and temperance and justice bind together heaven and earth and gods and men, and that this universe is therefore called Cosmos or Order, not disorder or misrule, my friend.

The rationalism of Socrates, however different from the heroic imagery of Homer and Hesiod, is still Greek and still heroic. Socrates, whom Alcibiades honored in Plato's *Symposium* for his heroism in battle, is primarily a hero of the intellect. He plunges into the agon of dialectic argument and emerges victor.

He uses the skill of mind to ascend beyond the shallow realm of the gods to what he believes to be a realm of unvarying and perfect truth. His is one of the great *itineraria mentis ad deum*, the use of human *arete*, or excellence, to achieve a godlike status. This is essentially an aristocratic doctrine of humanity. Few like Socrates are chosen to such powers of intellect to claim the very heart of divine wisdom as did he. Even with all his protestations of ignorance, even with the honor he paid to his divine *daimon* as a source of enlightenment, he champions the energetic search for knowledge rather than to leave his own soul dark and bound to rebirth in low-born men or even in animal bodies. The new hero for Socrates is not the lord of battles or the golden-tongued persuader; he is the philosopher-king, and he alone must rule amidst the confusion of the great masses of ordinary folk.

Had Judaism and Christianity never been, it is quite possible that the Greek ideas of the hero, alternating between Achilles and Socrates, would have dominated the Western world completely. This would have created a hierarchical structure not unlike the social structure of China under the ideal of Confucius. We might be more of one mind, East and West, although one cannot say whether we would be better or worse. But Abram came up out of Ur and the children of Israel out of Egypt. And that has made all the difference.

THE DIVINE COMEDY OF THE JUDAIC TRADITION

The adventures of the ancient leaders of Israel may have been told initially as hero tales like the epic of Gilgamesh. But by the time the stories came to be written down, they had passed through the covenant perspective of the Jewish monarchy. They had become a vast divine comedy in which God is the chief protagonist needing no heroic embellishment, claiming no heroic narrative details. And the men and women of the stories are not called to special skills or heroic self-assertion, but simply to obedience and trust.

The anti-heroism of the Bible is as much displayed by what is left out of the stories as by what is included. We might ask the many writers of the biblical narratives about a host of unfinished stories, loose ends, or faint suggestions of hero tales. We ask these questions not in criticism, but in order to clear the way for the positive emphases enshrined in the details of the biblical anti-heroes.

For instance, where did Adam go after his Michelangelesque expulsion from Paradise? Had Sophocles written the story, he might have dwelt upon the fact that Eve was Adam's daughter as well as his wife and that his sons by this issue were tainted by incest. Sophocles might have seen the murder of Abel as the logical consequence of the unnatural origin of the sons of Adam. He might have depicted the aged Adam as a refugee in a hostile earth, guided by the sorrowing Eve and cursing his warring sons. Or Aeschylus might have taken the figure of Cain and built him into a God-defying civilization hero like Prometheus, telling us more explicitly how the sons of Cain, in deadly enmity to all the shepherding sons of Abel, invented agriculture, settled cities with houses and public buildings, devised instruments of music and weapons of war. And of course these achievements would not have been possible without the taming of fire to human uses. How Sophocles might have wept for the exiled Hagar and her baby Ishmael! And what a tale might have been told of Ishmael's upbringing in the wilderness and of his return for vengeance against his weak and supplanting half-brother, Isaac! Would Homer have had the mighty hunter Esau allow his scheming brother, Jacob, to escape into exile, much less return in peace to the land and power he had stolen? Or imagine Homer dealing with the odyssey of Joseph. Joseph might have escaped from his slave-trading masters on the journey to Egypt and returned in secret to the homeland of Canaan, his Ithaca, after many heroic exploits in the terrible Sinai wilderness. Or he might have used superior intelligence and power to plan and execute the slaughter of his murderous brothers. And his father, Jacob, might have gone down mourning into Sheol for the utter decimation of his many sons in internecine warfare.

None of the stories we have so far mentioned even begin to exploit what the Greeks would have considered to be their heroic possibilities and the tragic consequences that would have followed from them. Perhaps Moses is the first true "hero" of Israel. He is a master of mighty exploits, a proven leader, and the founder of the people of the covenant as a great nation. The memory of Moses is especially cherished because of his critical role as founder. But nothing can establish him as a hero in a Greek sense. He is born a foreign slave in spite of his noble upbringing. After his one swift heroic act in slaying the Egyptian overseer on a Hebrew work gang, he is content to flee and become, presumably for life, a wilderness sheepherder married to a desert country girl. His first response to God's initiative in commanding him to go to Pharaoh to champion the freedom of his people is one of incredulity and massive self-doubt. Only when shored up by magical tricks and the promise of help from on high and from his brother, Aaron, does he consent to return to the Egyptian court. God performs the miracles of the plagues and the Sea of Reeds, Moses being only the mediator. Moses rises to considerable political stature in his shepherding of the recalcitrant refugees through the terrors and privations of the Sinai. But at the critical moment of God's wrath because of the building of the golden calf, Moses supervises the slaughter of 3,000 of his people for their sin. Then Moses behaves in a most un-Greek-like fashion: He offers himself as a substitutionary sacrifice. And unlike Zeus, Jehovah moderates his wrath, but not until he has brought a punitive plague upon the people. In crisis after crisis when the people murmur against Moses, he appeals to God, and God, not Moses, brings about the resolution of the crisis through judgment and mercy. When Moses wearies under the political complexities of his role as judge, his father-in-law, Jethro, provides the saving advice that the authority of judgment ought to be divided among many. Moses' greatest courage is his willingness to come face to face with God in the thunder and lightning of Mount Sinai, where the author describes God's presence as "like a devouring fire." Compare this with the highly companionable and conspiratorial relationship between Odysseus and Athena when she meets him in secrecy on his return to Ithaca. Together they devise his revenge and his reinstatement as king. Moses is a seer, a lawgiver, a mediator of the will of God, but not a hero in Greek style. He does not die tragically but in the fullness of old age, after having been given a mystical vision of the Promised Land from the mountaintop above the river Jordan.

Most of the key mediators of the Judaic divine comedy live to ripe old age. They are not required to pursue any code of personal honor. They are not required to risk their lives for personal gain. Not until the suicide of Saul is a character central to the main theme of the drama found to die in his or her prime. The death of Abel is not a subject of a tragic dynamic beyond the cursing of Cain. All those characters before and after Saul who are potentially the source of tragic drama—characters such as Ishmael and Hagar, Esau, Simeon, Jonathan, Uriah the Hittite, Bathsheba, plus many more—are quietly sent into literary oblivion as being of no more use to the sacred history once they have died. Samson's story is tragic, but it is the tragi-comedy of a powerful, somewhat lovable braggadocio; its presence in the Bible is puzzling and appears more as a kind of gargoyle canto offering a certain relief from the seriousness of the main line of the narrative, much like the gravedigger scene in Shakespeare's *Hamlet*.

Before dismissing the concepts of heroism and tragedy from the Old Testament, we should pay some attention to the potentially heroic ethos of ancient Israel during the gradual rise of Jewish nationalism, from the conquests of Joshua to the high tide of empire under the rule of King David. I select a few narrative details in this long story, details chosen for the purpose of weighing the possible presence of a heroic ethos in Israel and Judah.

At the risk of stating the obvious, note that the stories of the conquest of Canaan and the consolidation of Israel and Judah under one kingdom were written after the fact and were generally told as object lessons in piety rather than as military sagas. They may have been oral hero tales in the beginning. But in the literary tradition, we need not be surprised to find the heroic elements played down and the role of God as Lord of a covenanted people emphasized.

There is a major distinction between the tales of the patriarchs and the histories of Joshua, Judges, and Kings: What is new in the latter period is the necessity to use military force as a direct support for the ethos of the covenant. The people must fight; they can no longer run away. They are subject to all the temptations of pillage and ethical license characteristic of all wars. They also have to develop some degree of personal and national honor as well as military pride in this phase of their history. Yet the written record pointedly avoids the adoption of any overall heroic stance, even in the most triumphant days of King David. The King does not require a twenty-one-gun salute for himself; instead, he dances before the Ark of the Covenant dressed as a commoner.

The story of Joshua's entrance into the land of Canaan is an extension of the atmosphere of divine miracle that pervades the Mosaic sagas. Before crossing the Jordan, Joshua reminds the people of the divine promise of a large territory on condition that all the people keep all the commandments of the Law given to Moses. The river is miraculously turned back, the people cross dry-shod in a reenactment of the crossing of the Sea of Reeds, and the event is marked by twelve pillars of stone representing the twelve tribes. Similar stones are set up in the encampment at Gilgal, and the narrator reports that these events took the heart out of the Canaanites and the Amorites and put them in fear of the advancing Israelites. Jericho falls by a divine rather than military stratagem, where the sound of the shofar and the shouting of the people prove to be more swiftly effective than the Greeks' cumbersome wooden horse at Troy. When Achan, the Israelite, is reported to have taken some personal spoils at Jericho (in contrast to the spoils dedicated to the service of God), this otherwise normal heroic behavior is interpreted as putting a curse upon the people and serves to explain to them their initial defeat in the expedition against the city of Ai. With the destruction of these spoils and the spoiler, Achan, it is claimed that Joshua returns to Ai and destroys it utterly. After this battle, apparently not wanting to repeat the sin of Achan at Jericho, Joshua assembles all the people and makes them listen to every word of the law of Moses from beginning to end.

One should take note, however, that a slightly heroic note creeps into the story of the Ai campaign when the narrator gives some of the details of the ambush used against the army of the King of Ai. But for the most part Joshua's story is a continuing stream of divine miracles, in the telling of which the details of conventional military strategy become relatively unimportant. Thus the defeat of the five kings of the Amorites told in Joshua 10 depends upon the sun's standing still, while God lets loose a barrage of hailstones, but only on the enemy. Apparently God sometimes rains only on the unjust. Joshua is represented as attributing the Israelite military superiority solely to God's power. His farewell speech given to the people in his old age contains this portentous observation: "One of you puts to flight a thousand, since it is the Lord your God who fights for you as he promised you. Be very careful, therefore, to love the Lord your God" (Joshua 23:10-11). Joshua then cautions his people against intermarriage with the Canaanites and against adopting any of their customs and habits. A second source in Joshua 24 gives a similar farewell speech, when Joshua, having gathered the tribes at Shechem, rehearses the entire history of Israel, beginning with God's call to Abraham "from beyond the Euphrates to Canaan" (Joshua 24:2). In this speech Joshua states the essentially nonheroic formula that runs throughout the Old Testament military narratives: "It was not by your sword or by your bow. I gave you a land on which you had not labored, and towns that you had not built, and you live in them; you eat the fruit of vineyards and oliveyards that you did not plant" (Joshua 24:12-13). Joshua then pledges the people to an absolute obedience to their austere covenant and goes so far as to be highly suspicious of their promises of obedience. Against their protestations of loyalty, he sets up a huge stone under an oak at Shechem, saying, "See, this stone shall be a witness against us; for it has heard all the words of the Lord that he spoke to us; therefore it shall be a witness against you, if you deal falsely with your God" (Joshua 24:27). Here is the epitome of the ancient Jewish belief that human power, whether in war or in peace, is consequent not upon skill and cleverness, but upon a righteous response to God's law.

One might argue that the ancient song of Deborah in Judges 5 contains hints of heroic content such as her cursing of the tribes who refrained from opposing Sisera, the general of King Jabin of Hazor, and her triumphant description of the spoils gained from the rout of Sisera's army. But she is also careful to note, "by the waters of Megiddo; they got no spoils of silver. The stars fought from heaven, from their courses they fought against Sisera" (Judges 5:19-20). One must also reflect that the final defeat of Sisera is his ignominious slaughter at the hands of a woman who drives a tent peg through his head. The Greek tragedians make the slaughter of Agamemnon in his bath and by a woman a matter of major reproach to his own partisans, such that the woman who kills him is later slaughtered by her own children. In the Old Testament story, Jael, the killer of Sisera, is described as "of tent-dwelling women most blessed" (Judges 5:24). Victory is not confused with masculine pride. If God chooses a woman to administer the coup de grace, then "blessed is she."

Is Gideon a hero? We note that he follows the typical Jewish pattern of seeking to avoid the command of God when an angel orders him to rid the people of the marauding Midianites. In Judges 6 Gideon's first response to the angel's salute, "you mighty warrior," is not to preen himself but to dispute it. He argues against his divine commission by asking how the Lord, who has brought them out of Egypt, can abandon them to the ravages of the Midianites. The angel insists that Gideon can save Israel if he will but "go in thy might." But Gideon in essence answers, "I am no Achilles." That is, he emphasizes his low-brow status and general unfitness for the job, saying, "My clan is the weakest in Manasseh, and I am the least in my family" (Judges 6:15). In a recapitulation of the form of God's commission to Moses from the burning bush, Gideon requires a miraculous sign—and gets it—before agreeing to lead the people. Once convinced that God is with him, Gideon moves without hesitation. He divides his potential forces and takes a group of three hundred men from his army. As in the conquest of Ai by Joshua, so the battle against Midian is won by a ruse rather than by brute force; the enemy, hearing three hundred trumpets blare by night, think they are beset by a huge host. In panicked flight and mistaken self-slaughter, they are put to rout. Gideon dies in revered old age, having refused the offer of a kingship after his victory, saying, "I will not rule over you, and my son will not rule over you; the Lord will rule over you" (Judges 8:23). Thus Gideon breaks a principal rule of the Greek heroic ethos, namely, that all military victories must be consolidated and maintained by political power.

When we come to the story of Saul, we have the nearest equivalent in the Hebrew Bible to a heroic and tragic drama Greek style. I read the story as describing a good and generous-hearted man, who by virtue of a certain tragic flaw, comes to death by suicide in the midst of military defeat. In some ways Saul's drama fits the Aristotelian canon for tragedy. Although he is not a nobleman by birth, he is noble in bearing. Perhaps the most heroic description of a man in the Bible is this one-sentence statement about Saul in 1 Samuel, a sentence that would have called forth a recurring epithet and several lines from Homer: "There was not a man among the people of Israel more handsome than he; he stood head and shoulders above everyone else" (1 Samuel 9:2). Here is a kind of natural nobleman. And there is no doubt about the nobility of his purposes: his selfless courage in opposing the enemies of Israel; his kindness to his men and even to some of his enemies; and finally, his touching willingness to detach himself from wrath and show mercy, from time to time, to his antagonist, David.

What is Saul's tragic flaw? The Bible states it explicitly when, in the later source for the narrative, Samuel expresses displeasure that Saul has allowed his men to take spoils from the defeated Amalekites, contrary to the Lord's command. This late source makes it plain that Saul was doomed to lose the crown to David because of this breach of divine commandment. What Greek conquerors took for granted—the right to pillage as a reward for the burdens and pain of war—is Saul's undoing, or perhaps we should say, Samuel's chance to undo him. But the earlier author of the story has the nearest equivalent to Homeric style in the Bible. This earlier version of the story shows Saul as a kind of hero. His tragic flaw is the lightning of his passion (not Samuel's or the Lord's displeasure). His passion works for his good when he suddenly musters the army of Israel with the fragments of a slaughtered ox in response to the enemy's threat to blind the people of Jabesh-gilead. It also works for his good in his ecstatic prophecy on his way to Gilgal, but it almost destroys him when he condemns his own son, Jonathan.

The fatal side of Saul's passion is his deep melancholy, the flaw that first brings David into his court as a healing musician, that later estranges him from David by the pangs of jealousy, that still later drives him to consult a sorceress and to take his own life on the field of battle. From a literary point of view, it may be regrettable that Saul's story has been so drastically altered to depress him at the end by moral guilt and thus make way, as it were, for the rise of David. But the editors who made these changes were well in line with the anti-heroic stance of biblical narration. And even the original author is more Hebrew than Greek. Thus Saul, in a recapitulation of Gideon's self-doubt, chides Samuel for wanting to anoint him king, saying, "I am only a Benjaminite, from the least of the tribes of Israel, and my family is the humblest of all the families of the tribe of Benjamin. Why then have you spoken to me in this way?" (1 Samuel 9:21). No Greek ever disparaged his own lineage in this fashion. And how totally unaristocratic is the little detail that Saul has to borrow money from his servant in order to pay Samuel to divine the whereabouts of their lost asses? When Saul is about to be crowned king, he hides himself among the baggage of the people and has to be dragged out into his acceptance of power. But for all his modesty, he is one of the truly mighty men of Israel. And there is a tragic dignity in his death and in the companion-suicide of his armor bearer. There is also a heroic note at the very end of 1 Samuel when the men of Jabesh-gilead, whose city Saul had saved in his first military action, rescue the beheaded bodies of Saul and Jonathan from desecration on the wall of Beth-shan in the city of the Philistines. The men of Jabesh-gilead go in jeopardy of their lives to give Saul and Jonathan honorable burial, just as the Greeks rescue the body of Patroclus from the Trojans.

What shall we say of David, the most likely candidate in all of Israel for the title of hero? He cannot and does not boast of any famous lineage. He is the youngest son of his shepherd father, Jesse. Like Joseph, Moses, Gideon, and Saul before him, he is brought out of obscurity and the wilderness. He happens into the royal court as a musician. He stumbles into military prominence as a porter carrying food to his brothers in Saul's army. In 1 Samuel when he naively offers to take up the challenge of the Philistine giant Goliath, Saul offers to lend him his own armor. This brings a ludicrous note to the tale, quite unbecoming to the heroic literature of the Greeks, when we see David staggering around in the ill-fitting armor of the mighty Saul. Surely there are guffaws among the onlookers, and David may well take the armor off not simply because it encumbers him but also because it makes him a laughingstock.

Homer would give us the full context of this little episode; the biblical writers choose to brush past it with a light touch. In cleverness rather than strength, David defeats the giant Goliath.

David is no Achilles. But there is something of Odysseus in him, a "man of many wiles." He is capable of living the life of a wilderness marauder, both befriending and later threatening the house of Nabal. Later he actually hires himself out as a mercenary to the Philistine king, Achish. As the Greeks of old might have done, when David is king, he takes to his bed another man's wife because she pleases him. And even though she happens to be married to one of his best mercenaries, Uriah the Hittite, David does not hesitate to cover his tracks by a ruse that leads to the tragic death of Uriah. After Saul's death, David's officer, Abner, tries to support a son of Saul in opposition to David's bid for the crown. When David's general, Joab, murders Abner, David acts with shrewd political astuteness, making a great public display of his grief for Abner's death, just as he has mourned publicly for the deaths of Saul and Jonathan. I cannot believe that Abner dies contrary to David's will. But his open mourning for Abner pleases the people and absolves David in their minds from any hint of murder. Similarly, when David's rival and Abner's protege, Ishbaal, son of Saul, is murdered in his bed, David mourns in righteous indignation for this ignominious death of his own enemy. He goes so far as to slay those in his own party who thought to do him a favor by this killing. In these and other details, we see David's Odysseus-like character, his crafty, often immoral political instinct contrasting considerably with the open-hearted character of Saul.

The magnificently told story in 2 Samuel of David and Bathsheba, climaxing with the death of Bathsheba's and David's child, is presented by the narrator as the first stage of David's divine punishment for his crimes of adultery and murder. This story strikes me as the heart of the David saga. David has been warned by Nathan, the prophet, that because of his sins, the sword shall never depart from his house. How the Greeks would have wrung salt tears and bloody revenge for the double tragedy of Bathsheba in the deaths of her husband and her child! But with quiet dignity, the biblical story looks beyond her feelings to the fortunes of God's kingdom in this one simple verse: "Then David consoled his wife Bathsheba, and went to her, and lay with her, and she bore a son, and he named him Solomon. The Lord loved him" (2 Samuel 12:24).

The Hebrew habit of looking forward in hope to the future of the whole people of the covenant rather than behind in wrath toward their individual sins is characteristic of the whole divine comedy of the Old Testament. God's plan for Israel is far more important than individual human honor and revenge. Better a nation with an able but morally flawed king than a nation torn to pieces by revenge of these royal flaws. Note also that David is painted as being filled with guilt for his personal sins. He knows that he has incurred God's wrath and that the good destiny of his kingdom will not spare him personal grief, repentance, and divine punishment. So during the terrible rebellion of his son, Absalom, David flees his own capital, moved not by heroic self-righteousness, but in repentance for his sins and in horror of internecine warfare. His repentance becomes clear when he is reviled and pelted with stones by the hostile Shimei, a man of Saul's house, along the road of his retreat. His men ask whether they should not hack Shimei to pieces. David replies that Shimei is acting by the will of the Lord and implies that even Absalom's rebellion is part of the same divine vengeance against him.

I have suggested that David's grief for the death of Abner is more apparent than real, more political than personal. However, David is capable of grieving for his friends and is severely wracked in grief for the death of his son and enemy, Absalom. He gives his men orders to "deal gently" with his son, should they be able to capture him. But despite his wishes, the prisoner, Absalom, is deliberately slain. David's grief totally overcomes any impulse to heroic vengeance. When he returns to Jerusalem as the undisputed monarch of all of Israel and Judah, he pardons all his former enemies, even Shimei, who has publicly cursed him. He takes into his house Mephibosheth, the lame son of Jonathan, son of Saul, and shows him a special kindness.

David's career is filled with danger and bloodshed from beginning to end. Yet the writers of the story, while confessing many of the sordid details of his life, paint him as brave, generous-hearted, and one who above all fears God and in repentance seeks to return to God's commandments. The rule of this amorally fallible but persistently faithful king is remembered as a fulfillment, not as a disaster. The name of David is one of the most honored names in Jewish history. But his chroniclers do not cast him as a hero. It would have been his preference to follow the dark road of Saul and to die in place of his son, Absalom.

From these many details of the Hebraic ideal type, we can identify the characteristic marks of the biblical anti-hero. First, they come out of obscurity, without emphasis on aristocratic, much less divine, lineage. For the most part, they are not the first-born, despite the emphasis in antiquity upon the law of primogeniture. Isaac is younger than his brother Ishmael; Jacob is younger than Esau; Judah is fourth in line; Joseph is younger than all but one of his eleven brothers; and David is the youngest of all his brothers.

The choice of these unlikely champions is not due to their own ambition; it is rather ascribed to the initiative of God. That is to say, they do not rise to immortal remembrance by virtue of their own will to power. They are called to their task as mediators of God's will to help to fulfill the divine comedy of an entire people.

They not only lack personal ambition but also prefer obscurity, at least at the beginning. Abraham chooses to hide his identity as Sarah's husband when Pharaoh dangerously covets her for himself. Jacob has a serious inner and outer struggle at the ford of Jabbok before acceding to God's command to take possession of his inheritance in the Promised Land. Moses pleads rhetorical ineptitude as his reason for not wanting to confront Pharaoh with the demand to release his people from slavery. Gideon and Saul consider themselves unfit for leadership, and David is in no way a candidate for royalty in the mind of his father, Jesse, or in his own mind. Only Noah and Abraham seem to respond immediately and without protest to the mighty missions laid upon them from on high.

Once committed to their divinely ordained role, the major figures in the Old Testament do not need to develop any special skills or excellence to fulfill God's command. The biblical narrative describes in detail the dimensions of Noah's ark, but no one bothers to say or explain how it happens that Noah is a carpenter or shipbuilder. Even Joseph looks lightly upon the many native gifts he uses to rise to high political eminence in Egypt. The Greek authors would have filled in those amazing blanks, noting in detail why Joseph is such a successful administrator in the house of Potiphar and in prison, how he comes to have the art of dream interpretation, and how he ingratiates himself in the royal Egyptian court. Joseph's rise to power is not the focus of the story, only the means by which the people of the covenant survive their sins as well as a great famine and how they become a great multitude in Egypt. David and Saul are obviously military geniuses, but we have in the Bible only a few slim details of their skills and tactics. The same is true of Joshua and Gideon. In all these cases, God's power is the center of focus. Human success is given as a direct consequence of righteousness toward God rather than the disciplined development of skill. Certainly Elijah knew nothing about the art of burning water-soaked sacrifices, even though that is his most signal achievement. In sum, they all seem to take no particular pride in their work as such. They do not become as gods as the Greek heroes aspire to do. They would be horrified by the common Greek epithet *godlike* if it were applied to any of them as it is applied to many of the Greek heroes. Rather they are content to be revealers and mediators of a power that transcends them.

The chief Jewish virtue is obedience, submission to God, including a crucial willingness to repent and return to God whenever they are disobedient. As in the case of King David, they seem to welcome misfortune as purging them from previous sins, just so long as God does not abandon the people. I have particular sympathy for the agonized life of the patriarch Jacob. He spends most of his years mourning the supposed death of his favorite son, Joseph. His hope for the success of the covenanted community is meager, given the incest of his firstborn, Reuben, the violence of his sons Simeon and Levi against Shechem, and the adultery of his fourthborn, Judah, with Tamar. All of these tales suggest that Jacob is a man whose faith in his divine comedy persists in spite of overwhelming inducements to despair. It is not surprising that in his one audience with Pharaoh, in Genesis 47, he describes his 130 years as "few and evil." He has lived, as Job says, "swifter than a weaver's shuttle," (Job 7:6) and there was no satisfaction in all those years until the reuniting of his family in Egypt. Yet by Joseph's long exile, the people of the covenant are saved from external destruction and internal dissolution. And that alone was significant to the writers of the story.

With the exception of the empire builders Joshua and his successors, these biblical leaders are all men of peace, not of war. Again Jacob comes to mind as the dweller in tents, living under the domination of his mother. How unlike his brother Esau he is, the hunter and warrior whom the father, Isaac, seems to admire because he does not have these robust qualities himself. But the Bible implies that Esau, firstborn of Isaac, is not chosen for the patriarchal role precisely because he is too heroic in the Greek sense. God needs men of peace. Rebekkah knows this and skillfully arranges for Jacob to receive the primary blessing of his father. Also, by her adroit management, Jacob is temporarily exiled during the period of Esau's wrath.

All the so-called great men of the Hebrew Bible, from Noah, Abraham, and the patriarchs to the builders of empire through

Solomon, with the one exception of King Saul, live to old age. These "success stories" belong to a steady divine comedy. These leaders see the fruits of their labors, despite immense hardships and frequent tragedies that burden them along the way. They are obviously beloved and revered for their simple yet burdensome endurance in faith. And for this quality, which is repeatedly correlated with the favor of God and the persistence of their community in history, they are chiefly remembered. David's temple is gone, but his name and the city that bears his name (City of David) endure to this day.

Judaic Mythology in Modern Christianity

VOLUMES COULD BE WRITTEN on the ways in which the literature of the Greek classics, Judaic history, and Christian biblical faith combined to produce the broad dimensions of modern Western civilization. Modern science and all its derivatives are more the children of Hellenic rationalism than of Judaic faith. On the other hand, Judaic messianism—with its hope for a transformation of the earth into a sacred kingdom of righteousness and justice—is the source of Western dreams of progress, in contrast to the basically tragic philosophies of history in Hellenic thought and feeling.

Ideally we should consider ourselves as equal beneficiaries of Athens and Jerusalem, yet in doing so we must overcome Tertullian's famous denunciation from *Prescriptions Against Heretics*:

> What has Jerusalem to do with Athens, the church with the academy, the Christian with the Heretic? Our principles come from the Porch of Solomon, who had himself taught that the Lord is to be sought in simplicity of heart. I have no use for a Stoic or a Platonic or a dialectic Christianity. After Jesus Christ we have no need for speculation, after the Gospel no need for research. When we come to believe, we have no desire to believe anything else; for we begin by believing that there is nothing else for which we have to believe.

Contrary to Tertullian's rhetorical question, the heritages of the two cities have had much to do with each other. The Christian churches (especially Protestant Christianity) have been a major source of egalitarian and democratic values. The academy has been the major stimulus of our scientific-technological progress toward a longer and better quality of human life. The nineteenth century in Europe and America represented the high tide of human inventiveness, supported by a strong faith in the democratic progress of humanity onward and upward forever. But today, after the end of the twentieth century with its many wars and depravities of human behavior, we face a darker horizon, a less hopeful and nearly tragic sense of the shape of human history. In the modes of secularism, we are more nearly Greek. In the modes of Christianity, the hope for human fulfillment tends more and more to be postponed to the hereafter as the world appears to drift toward Armageddon.

Judaic messianism looked for a new earth, not a substitution of a new heaven for a corrupted earth. The phenomena of Jesus' life and ministry transformed their messianic role into that of the suffering servant, not the conquering hero. He became but one instance among many in the Judaic history of persecuted servants of God who, in the name of divine justice on earth, challenged what Paul called "principalities and powers, against the rulers of darkness of this world, against spiritual wickedness in high places" (Ephesians 6:12). It is no accident that the earliest Christians were Jews whose initial aim was to purify their own faith and practice, not to establish a new religion. These circumstances lead me to urge a perspective toward Christianity as a faith continuing and enhancing its Jewish origins, but not transcending them.

In this effort I mean no disrespect toward our classical Greco-Roman heritage. But there is a kind of Homeric hubris deeply planted in Western culture from the beginning—a glorification of war and conflict with a persistent undercurrent of tragedy and despair—that needs some kind of check and balance from a biblical perspective. In the corporate and collective dimensions of modern societies, an often brutal heroic rivalry is very much alive. We continue to live in an age of rival nationalisms where the preservation of national honor is more important than national righteousness or international cooperation. We live in an age when the powerful of the earth have occupied, conquered, and pillaged so-called backward nations, with the naïve moral assumption that it is our manifest destiny to civilize those whom we exploit. The Greeks saw themselves as superior to all other tribes, whom they called barbarians. The "barbarians" eventually put the Greeks and Romans back into the shadows of antiquity. The English at one time looked down upon "lesser breeds without the law," that is, without their law and folkways, and the British Empire is no more. Germany twice strove to be *über Alles*, which brought about two major tragedies in scarcely more than one generation. Now the United States is faced with the burden of being "the greatest nation on earth," as well as the uneasy police force of the world.

To counteract the foregoing trends, I believe that our Christian heritage needs a shift in the direction of its Judaic origins. In the development of Christian orthodoxy, we have lost some of the Judaic wisdom and energy from which Christianity originally sprang. We should observe more carefully the parallels between the stories of the major figures and prophets of the Hebrew Bible and those told of Jesus' struggle "against the rulers of darkness of this world."

In Luke 2 an angel announces to Mary that she is pregnant with a son, saying, "... the Lord God will give to him the throne of his ancestor David. He will reign over the house of Jacob forever, and of his kingdom there will be no end" (Luke 2:33). Although Mary is already espoused to Joseph of the house of David, their marriage has not yet been consummated. Consequently, Mary cannot think of herself as pregnant, much less dream of having such a son. Her hesitation is gentle and lowly until the angel argues, "For nothing will be impossible with God" (Luke 2:37). Only then does Mary respond, "Here am I, the servant of the Lord; let it be with me according to your word" (Luke 2:38).

Here is a typically Hebraic lack of personal ambition combined with the acceptance of whatever fate is believed to derive from divine initiative. As the story of Jesus unfolds, the pattern repeats the Hebraic biblical motifs of unlikely origin and threatened tragedy. The child is born in a stable for lack of any humane lodging. While still an infant, his native country is plagued by a scourge of infanticide, forcing his family to become refugees driven to a foreign land. Jesus' major inspirations and calling, like those of Abraham, come from the wilderness, not from established tradition or political leverage: first, from the preaching and baptism of a countercultural rebel and outcast, John the Baptist; and second, from a wilderness encounter with Satan tempting him to assume a messianic role even greater than that prophesied to his mother. Does Jesus go into the wilderness in grief and in order to find himself after the murder of John? When in his loneliness he accepts John's role and rejects Satan's, is this a kind of death of one life and resurrection to another? From these events grow his charisma, his power of healing, all treated not as skills that he has perfected but as divine gifts. For those who follow him without fear of the hostility of priests and Roman overlords, he is a man of peace par excellence. He neither seeks nor collaborates with military or political power. The tragedy of Jerusalem moves him to tears, not to rebellion. And whereas Socrates answered his accusers with ten thousand well-chosen words, Jesus stands before Pilate in passive silence. He allows himself to be a victim; he gives himself to the cross after promising his disciples that he will always be with them through the might and justice of God.

In these many ways, Jesus was a true Jew, reliving the ordeals and triumphs of his ancestors without pride of accomplishment or hunger for fame. The endings of the Gospel stories of Jesus' life are mainly responsible for a major break from Judaism and a major thrust toward a new religion. The early Christian community believed that he literally came back to life and was endowed with messianic authority in his Father's kingdom. This led quickly to the faith that Jesus' primary messianic role was to guarantee personal immortality to all who believed in him. They also came to believe that at some later time he would return to the world in a monarchial mode and establish a new Kingdom of God on earth in full and undiluted peace and power.

Unitarian Universalists like me and possibly many Protestants must question the literal credibility of the resurrection narratives. I cannot believe that this man so cruelly slain, so obviously dead and entombed, came alive again. On the other hand, one need not expunge the miracles of the New Testament simply because they are literally unbelievable. What really grips my heart and mind about the Easter stories is not what happened to Jesus, but what happened to those who continued to love him. Even if no one actually saw him alive, even if those tales of his bodily resurrection are the make-believe of an adoring community written down long after his death, the chief story within these stories is the resurrection of his loving and grieving survivors. That is what seizes my imagination. The Gospels present us with a treasury of mythic poetry that continues, without replacing, the outlook on life of their Judaic origins. What follows is a way of reading the post-crucifixion narratives, a way of saving truths buried in mythical vehicles, a way in which a contemporary church might genuinely celebrate Easter without a sacrifice of intellect.

I approach the resurrection stories by a flashback in the Gospel narratives to an earlier event. Jesus spent most of his young life in northern Palestine, far from the holy city of David, Jerusalem. We learn that he went as far north as Caesarea Philippi, close under the shadow of Mount Hermon, an area very near to what we now call the Golan Heights. There it was, for perhaps the only time in his ministry, that Jesus lost his temper with one of his disciples, Peter. Jesus was famous as a country preacher, healer, and miracle worker. All kinds of fanciful stories were circulating about him. How natural of him to want to take a kind of public-opinion poll by asking his disciples at Caesarea Philippi, "Who do people say that the Son of Man is?" (Matthew 16:13). Notice that he calls himself the Son of Man, which in his native Aramaic language means simply, a man, a son of the human race. But his disciples answer with a confusing set of titles, some of which appear superstitious, namely, John the Baptist, Elijah, Jeremiah, and "one of the prophets." Elijah and Jeremiah were dead. Although John the Baptist may have been a mentor to Jesus, there are no historical or mythological reasons to confuse Jesus with the man who had publicly baptized him and who was murdered by Herod. Only the title "one of the prophets," meaning a new prophet, might fit. One can see Jesus fixing his disciples with a fierce and unavoidable gaze, and demanding,

> "But who do you say that I am?" Simon Peter answered, "You are the Messiah, the Son of the living God." And Jesus answered him, "Blessed are you, Simon son of Jonah! For flesh and blood has not revealed this to you, but my Father in heaven."
>
> —Matthew 16:15–17

This is both a shocking answer and a loving answer. The Greek *Christos* is equivalent to the Jewish *Messiah*, a conquering divine hero who, in the Jewish faith of the time, is to assume control over the nations and to establish on earth and in the hearts of all people the law of God and a kingdom of everlasting peace. Is this young Galilean peasant preacher, Jesus, that Messiah? Thus Peter's answer is shocking with respect to the Messiah part. Is he the son of the living God? This is more likely, since the Jews had always regarded themselves as all the children of God. This is the loving part of Peter's answer. Jesus blesses Peter for this judgment, thereby seeming to accept some kind of messianic role. Is Jesus a megalomaniac when he answers, "Blessed are you, Simon son of Jonah! For flesh and blood has not revealed this to you, but my Father in heaven"? He seems to say, "Right, I am Messiah, but not by any evidence you have seen, only by a kind of divine intuition." Then Jesus proceeds to unpack that intuition, first cautioning all the disciples to keep it a secret. Matthew writes, "From that time on, Jesus began to show his disciples that he must go to Jerusalem and undergo great suffering at the hands of the elders and chief priests and scribes, and be killed, and on the third day be raised. And Peter took him aside and began to rebuke him, saying, 'God forbid it, Lord! This must never happen to you'" (Matthew 16:21-22).

What a disappointment to Peter! Going to Jerusalem, that's fine. That's the proper city for the Messiah to start from. But to be killed and resurrected. Peter is shocked. What kind of Babylonian, Egyptian, non-Jewish superstitious nonsense is this? Peter rebukes him and says, "God forbid it, Lord! This must never happen to you." At this point Jesus loses his temper. He can foresee that if he goes to Jerusalem, it will be his destiny to suffer for his radical challenge to the temple establishment just as the prophets before him have suffered. Naturally he is afraid. And when Peter tempts him to conventional dreams of messianic glory without blood, sweat, tears, and death, Jesus recognizes his own temptation to the same wishful thinking. In great internal struggle and outward anger, having first praised Peter, he turns to him with fire in his eyes, saying:

> "Get behind me, Satan. You are a stumbling block to me; for you are setting your mind not on divine things but on human things." Then Jesus told his disciples, "If any want to become my followers, let them deny themselves and take up their cross and follow me. For those who want to save their life will lose it, and those who lose their life for my sake will find it. For what will it profit them if they gain the whole world but forfeit their life? Or what will they give in return for their life? For the Son of Man is to come with his angels in the glory of his father, and then he will repay everyone for what has been done."
> —Matthew 16:23-7

Is Jesus remembering his vision of the time in mountain soli-
tude when he heard Satan tempting him to seize control of the
whole world in exchange for his worship of Satan? And since
Satan was always reputed to be one who could work endlessly
through disguises, does Jesus have the temerity to accuse Peter of
serving as a satanic voice? Perhaps this fiery response is really ad-
dressed to himself. Peter has tempted him with a conventional
messianic role in which he would receive legions of angels to save
him from the Jerusalem ordeal. In any case, he resists all heroic
temptation and defines his role in the famous maxim of losing
one's life to save it.

Here is a radical redefinition of *Messiah*, not as a conquering
hero, but as one who comes first as a suffering servant, a martyred
prophet. It is obvious to me that the storytellers who wrote this
passage long after his death believed that he had returned to life,
that he was not simply a tragic Messiah, but rather their long expected divine Messiah and savior. In order to fulfill the messianic
prophesies of scripture, after his death he would have to reappear,
this time with his army of angels.

The entire structure of Christian orthodoxy (in contrast to
Jewish faith) rests on the literal belief in Christ's resurrection. The
question then comes, how does someone in our time who cannot
accept this kind of supernatural narrative make any sense out of
Christian theology? It can be done only by treating the Christian
narratives in the same way one reads the Judaic narratives: as a
kind of poetic mythology that reflects the heights and depths of
the human condition.

All four Gospels agree that Jesus' body is buried in a tomb
sealed by a great stone, that the body disappears from its burial
place, and that a living Jesus appears to several of his women followers and later to his disciples. They also agree that up to the moment of his reappearance, his ending is completely tragic. He has
refused to defend himself in his trial before the Roman authorities. He has been turned over to a mob thirsting for his death and

has been publicly humiliated, tortured, and slain. During these dread events, those who might have tried to defend him were totally dispirited and scattered. One disciple, Judas, betrayed him for money and in full despair took his own life even as Jesus' life was being taken. The only disciple who remained at all near him at his trial was Peter. Yet this very man who had sought to recognize him as Messiah and Savior, publicly denied any connection with him when challenged with possible guilt by association. The only ones who appeared to favor him in his final ordeal were the man who helped carry his cross, a few women, including his mother, who wept as they watched him die, and Joseph of Arimathaea who received Jesus' dead body and helped to place it in a tomb of his own.

I find it fascinating that Johann Sebastian Bach's two tremendous oratorios detailing these tragic events end as true tragedies, without the solace of resurrection faith. Of course, Bach had such a faith and expressed it repeatedly in many of his choral works written for the church. But he also made it possible for Christians and non-Christians alike to feel the depth of this tragedy unalloyed by hope. The powerful last chorus of his *St. Matthew Passion* uses as its text, "Here yet awhile sit we weeping."

What then can be the meaning today of such a narrative, in face of the incredibility of the assertion that Jesus returned to life? I hold that there is a great deal of meaning. Nor do I wish to argue that those who believe literally in the resurrection are wrong. Rather, I hold that the Bible is not theirs alone, that the Jewish Talmudic tradition of a variety of interpretations, often contrasting and contradictory, ought to be reverenced and not suppressed. What follows is one of many ways of finding the myths of the New Testament true to life even though they may appear untrue to fact. The Bible is too great a work of art to be confined to any single mode of meaning.

To demonstrate such a procedure, I shall turn to resurrection narratives in the Gospel of John. The other three Gospels begin their Easter story with a visit to Jesus' tomb by his mother, Mary, his friend Mary Magdalene, and others. John's narrative begins more simply: Only Mary Magdalene goes to the tomb the day after Jesus' burial, "early on the first day of the week when it was still dark" (John 20:1). What kind of gruesome errand is this? Perhaps like Antigone of old, this gutsy young woman wants to assure herself that no dishonor has been done to the corpse of him whom she most deeply loved. To her shock and dismay, the tomb is open and the body is gone. She runs and finds Peter and some of the other disciples, telling them this dismal news. Several of them, including the volatile Peter, who had been so quick to honor Jesus and equally quick to deny him, run with Mary and others back to the tomb. After seeing this terrible evidence of grave robbery, they go off, leaving Mary Magdalene alone, weeping in her grief. A man approaches her and asks her why she is weeping. At this moment the story is so stunningly written that I quote directly from it without paraphrase:

> Supposing him to be the gardener, she said to him, "Sir, if you have carried him away, tell me where you have laid him, and I will take him away." Jesus said to her, "Mary!" She turned and said to him in Hebrew, "Rabbouni!" (which means Teacher). Jesus said to her, "Do not hold on to me, because I have not yet ascended to the Father. But go to my brothers and say to them, "I am ascending to my Father and your Father, to my God and your God."
>
> —John 20:15-17

This stunning narrative has all the brevity, economy, depth, and weight that appear in the Genesis story of Abraham's near sacrifice to God of his son, Isaac. The word "Mary," the response "Rabbouni," the woman's rush to embrace, the raised hand and quiet command "Touch me not," all are in the highest tradition of biblical storytelling. Jesus seems to confirm the fact that he is dead and gone, but in the language of his Jewish ancestors, he also says, "I am about to be gathered to my Father who is also your Father, to my God who is also your God." Go to the men I loved and cared for, comfort them, tell them to be of good heart, for my God and my Father is also theirs.

The same strange Jesus then appears among a group of terror-stricken disciples who have shut themselves in a house for fear that the persecutors of Jesus might be looking for them. He gives them a blessing and says:

> "Peace be with you. As the Father has sent me, so I send you."
> When he had said this, he breathed on them and said to them, "Receive the Holy Spirit. If you forgive the sins of any, they are forgiven them; if you retain the sins of any, they are retained."
> —John 20:21,22

This is a kind of novel empowerment, with the purpose of purifying traditional Jewish law; it passes on to these people a way of humanizing their sense of covenant. It is a kind of democratic interpretation of sacred law that is understandably foreign to orthodox Judaism. However, it is a movement clearly within the covenanted community of Judaism.

But what about Peter and the other disciples who "went away again unto their own home"? John does not mention Peter's name again until the next and last chapter of his Gospel.

It turns out that several of the disciples including Peter had gone off to Galilee and the Sea of Galilee, several days journey from Jerusalem. I see the swift-running, quick-speaking Peter as exhausted, spiritually drained, and deeply depressed because of the empty tomb. Peter had found only emptiness, but no indication of resurrection. When they reach the Sea of Galilee, his first words to his friends are, "I am going fishing" (John 21:3). In other words, the sacred mission is dead, the Messiah, though promised to have risen, is no Messiah, nothing has changed. It was all a bad dream. Peter says by his action, "Let's try to pick up where we left off before this strange man called us into service. Let's go back to the simplicity and nonentity of the fisherman's life." They went in the evening into their boat and despondently fished all night without catching so much as one fish in their nets.

As the sun rose over the Jordanian mountains to the east and cast its early golden light on the west shore of the sea, they saw a man standing on that shore whom they did not recognize. John tells his readers that the man is Jesus. Even Jesus' voice is unrecognized when he calls out to them, "'Children, you have no fish, have you?' They answer him, 'No.' He says to them, 'Cast the net to the right side of the boat, and you will find some'" (John 21:5-6). Whereupon they make a huge catch. One of the other disciples says to Peter, "It is the Lord." And the impulsive Peter does exactly what one might expect: He jumps into the water and swims vigorously ashore. The others, Jesus or no Jesus, haul in the nets and bring their catch ashore. Jesus and Peter are already sitting at a fish fry on a campfire, and they invite the rest of the men to join in. The men are so frightened by this apparent ghost that in John's narration they never say a word.

Then Jesus begins a remarkable conversation with Peter, his major supporter and only betrayer other than Judas, by asking, "Do you love me?" Three times he asks and three times Peter replies "You know I do." Then Peter hears the fateful words reminiscent of the terrible Satan explosion at Caesarea Philippi:

> Very truly, I tell you, when you were younger, you used to fasten your own belt and to go wherever you wished. But when you grow old, you will stretch out your hands, and someone else will fasten a belt around you and take you where you do not wish to go.
>
> —John 21:18

John then explains to his readers that this was Jesus' prophecy of Peter's eventual martyrdom. Not anywhere in the Bible, but in extra-biblical legends of the Catholic Church, the story is told that Peter eventually arrived in Rome and founded the church there. He defied the Roman authorities and was condemned to crucifixion. But the Romans granted him one final wish, that he be crucified head down so that he might not appear or presume to rival his Lord. St. Peter, the volatile friend and weak betrayer of Jesus, seasoned and strengthened by Jesus' own martyrdom, had found the strength at last to follow like some old classical hero in his master's footsteps. This was indeed a major resurrection.

I do not quarrel with those who believe what I cannot believe, namely, the literal return to life of Jesus of Nazareth. In my reading, those who returned to the life he gave them did so dramatically, in contrast to Judas and perhaps others who were smitten to the core by the tragedy of his death. Peter did not remain in Galilee, a forgotten fisherman. He became a major apostle, arrived at his cross, and accepted it with true courage. And to that courageous woman Mary Magdalene, who had dared to come alone by night to guard his corpse, Jesus had spoken in a soothing and comforting spirit as if to say: Do not fret about my death and burial. But go to my brothers who are afraid and sorrowing. Tell them to take courage. Assure them that I am no poor ghost, doomed to haunt the places of my defeat, but that I live in their hearts as I live in the bosom of the Father who created me, as each of you will live after you die in the lives of your loving survivors and in the bosom of my Father who is also your Father. In brief, the resurrection is that of the disciples, who having suffered what seemed like the ultimate defeat, had a new life and spirit infused into them. This concept is expressed in the story of Pentecost, when the power that seems to belong to Jesus alone is suffused among those who receive from him a lasting change.

All that I say of these matters is heavily colored by my own presuppositions and biases over which I have no control, any more than the disciples were able to control their despair after the crucifixion. I do not presume to "explain" the miraculous accounts of Jesus' appearances after his death. Such experiences may have been common and expected two thousand years ago. They are less common but by no means unheard of today. If any friend of mine were to say, "I saw my dead mother last night," I would not argue with this alleged fact or try to explain it. And if they rejoiced in this post-mortem meeting, why shouldn't I? I have not seen either my father nor mother, nor two of my sons after their deaths. But the memories of my parents come to me constantly, with the affect always of comfort and encouragement. By a curious twist of fate, the memories of my deceased sons have the same salutary effect, almost as if they too were my ancestors rather than my descendants. Our bonds of love, which were often threatened during their lifetimes, remain now firm and undamaged. I see them only in the imaginations of my mind, but they are thus with me in a way that they were not always with me during their and my life together.

The German artist Kaethe Kollwitz, who lost a son in World War I and a grandson in World War II, once wrote, "Blessed are they who remember their fathers and mothers with gladness." And all over the world there are tribes east and west, in Asia, Polynesia, South America, Africa, and among Native Americans who honor their ancestors and hold them in gentle worship as a communal remembrance, as a way of strengthening and fructifying the living tribe. They know they would have had no life without those who brought them into life and who cared for them in the days of their youth. They seem to know that the good future of their society depends upon memories of those who went before them.

When one of my now deceased sons was a small boy, he came home from school one day and cheerfully announced to his Unitarian mother something he had been told by a Roman Catholic playmate, namely, "Jesus is the Son of God." To which she replied, "So are you, honey." And the two of them were satisfied and at peace with this good news.

The Incredible Folklore of Easter

What I call the folklore of Easter is that somewhat varied body of stories in the four Gospels describing a people's belief in Jesus' resurrection from death. It is truly folklore because it arose among the followers of Jesus as an oral tradition, a series of stories passed around from person to person for quite a few years before any of it was written down. And even after it was put into writing, this body of stories is not told with complete consistency. Nevertheless, it is an incredible folklore.

The word *incredible* has a double meaning in American English, one literal and the other poetic. The literal meaning is "unbelievable," and indeed for me the folklore of Easter is literally unbelievable. I do not believe that Jesus, after being truly killed, truly rose from the dead. I do not believe that this alleged resurrection confers immortality upon those who believe in it. It is a safe guess that most religious liberals share my skepticism.

But let us look at the poetic meanings of the word *incredible*, such as "marvelous," "wonderful," "better than one could ever hope." Enthusiastic people frequently resort to this poetic usage. Someone asks, "How was the concert?" and you reply, "incredibly great," meaning that its greatness was not false or untrue but wonderful beyond what you can understand or express. I claim that people whose religion is liberal, that is, free, are not bound to take any of our traditions literally. My understanding of the folklore is that it shows us a real wonder, namely, that many of the followers of Jesus emerged from their grief and depression into an active fellowship full of hope. For me the idea of the resurrection applies not to Jesus, but to the broken lives of those followers who eventually became the founders of the church. In making this assertion, I do not mean to deny that these followers did not believe literally in his bodily resurrection. I am sure they did. But we can appreciate their experience without having to share their literal belief.

Let us look at one example. In the Gospel of Matthew, the Gospel writer tells his resurrection story of Jesus immediately after his account of Jesus' burial.

> After the sabbath, as the first day of the week was dawning, Mary Magdalene and the other Mary went to see the tomb. And suddenly there was a great earthquake; for an angel of the Lord, descending from heaven, came and rolled back the stone and sat on it. His appearance was like lightning, and his clothing white as snow. For fear of him the guards shook and became like dead men. But the angel said to the women, "Do not be afraid; I know that you are looking for Jesus who was crucified. He is not here; for he has been raised, as he said. Come, see the place where he lay. Then go quickly and tell his disciples, 'He has been raised from the dead, and indeed he is going ahead of you to Galilee; there you will see him.' This is my message for you." So they left the tomb quickly with fear and great joy, and ran to tell his disciples. Suddenly Jesus met them and said, "Greetings!" And they came to him, took hold of his feet, and worshiped him. Then Jesus said to them, "Do not be afraid; go and tell my brothers to go to Galilee; there they will see me."
>
> —Matthew 28:1-10

Matthew's is the only Gospel that has the angel roll away the stone with the help of an earthquake. To me, a resident of the New

Madrid earthquake fault, where a major quake could occur any moment, this detail, along with the lightning-like vision of the angel, crackles with electricity even if it strains literal credulity. My second excitement comes from the narrator's comparison of the reactions of the two sets of living participants in this excitement. The women were terrified, but they stood their ground and listened. The soldiers, supposedly men of real courage, had the shakes and passed out.

Hidden in these swift details is a summary of some differences between men and women and of the unique relationship of the man, Jesus, to women. The male guardians of the tomb, as Matthew and other Gospel folklore state, have been ordered there so that no one would steal the body and then spread the false propaganda that Jesus has risen from the dead as he promised he would. The Roman governor has no interest in protecting this corpse except as it might be used for political purposes.

The women have gone there in grief, not expecting resurrection and knowing there is nothing they can do. As I read it, they are responding to the universal urge to visit the grave of a loved one. They have wept openly at the crucifixion, and like mothers and wives everywhere, they do not care or fear who notices their grief. To show grief is to keep alive a loss, not to bury it in denial.

When something like the combination of an earthquake and an angel arrives to blast away the great rock and threaten military control, the soldiers revert to the ultimate form of denial: They pass out. But the women, however natural their fears, have been hurt too much to let even an earthquake and an angel unhinge them. They stay and listen, and while they continue to be afraid, they also rejoice at the good news they believe they are given.

The soldiers in this story have lost nothing by the death of Jesus except their own post-crucifixion authority. But consider what the women have lost beyond the life of their friend. They live at a time when men completely dominate all the public and private sources of cultural order and meaning. They have no place in government, in family authority, even in religion. They cannot study the Torah; they cannot become rabbis, priests, or officials of any kind. Then Jesus came along treating them as equals, preaching to their experience as well as to the male population, using them in his parables, healing them and blessing their children and even using their children as examples of what it is like to belong to the Kingdom of Heaven. This incredible blessing from Jesus was extended to female prostitutes and male tax collectors at a time when both of these classes of people occupied approximately the same status as they do today in many cultures.

Here was a new world order for the women of Israel on a grand scale. Small wonder that a poor woman anointed Jesus with precious ointment on the eve of his martyrdom and that many women were prominent in the early years of the church. When Jesus died as a lynched criminal, it appeared to women, probably more vividly than to men, that they had not only lost a dear friend, they had lost a whole way of life.

In thinking about these things, I came to realize why I grieved more over the assassination of John Kennedy than I did over the death of my own brother in World War II. Kennedy was my age, my college classmate, and the embodiment of a new order of the ages arriving in the White House in the name of my generation. He boldly and cheerfully stood for a government that sought justice for victims of injustice. At the same time, he celebrated the beauty of life by bringing old Pablo Casals to play his miraculous cello in the President's living room. It was JFK who respected high intelligence in government, who rejoiced that it took many people of great intellect gathered in the White House dining room to match the wisdom of Thomas Jefferson when he had dined alone.

Thus, while the military guard at Jesus' tomb collapsed into total ineptitude, the women ran, not walked, to tell the disciples their story. And at first those men found that story literally incredible. I find that story poetically true. In gem-like compression, it expresses in the briefest space the human power of courage and hope to rise up in the midst of grief. It is the human analogy of the miracle of spring following winter. Taken literally, spring is no more than the result of a tilt of the earth toward the sun and the effects of water on buried roots and seeds or the effect of warmth on buds locked up within their frozen wintry state. Taken poetically, spring is an allegro dancing of flowers, a bursting of sunlight and a running of waters like the women who ran from the tomb to tell their good news.

What have some of our Christian brothers and sisters done with that story? They have robbed it of its poetry and have made it into a literal passport to immortality, saying that if Jesus could literally rise from the dead, so could they, thanks to him. Literalmindedness is a distortion of religion into some form of magic. If the folklore of resurrection means only a hope in a world utterly different from this one, what does that say but that this world is no good, this world is hopeless, without any enduring or renewable value. That is not what I mean by religion. That kind of Christian Easter is not the hope of the world: It is the counsel of despair and a yearning for compensatory magic. It is even more the counsel of despair when one understands the crucifixion literally as God's purchase of salvation and immortality for believers. How many tears have been shed for two millennia about that one death! This is the institutionalizing of grief, concentrating all grief on one person's death, while we send thousands of living men and women to war, and many more thousands of men, women, and children to their premature deaths, all the while singing "Onward, Christian Soldiers."

I know nothing of personal immortality, yes or no, good or bad. What I am sure of is that both heaven and hell exist all over this world, here and everywhere, and that a cynical expectation that earthly hell is the stronger of the two, the common rule, is an expression of despair. If the only answer and antidote to such evil is the expectation of a new heaven after death, then this is despair written large and ultimate.

I do not and must not blame anyone who, unlike me, is in such deep pain that their only hope is for death and immortality, especially those who have earned the right to look beyond this world, so painful to them, toward a transcendent fulfillment. But I honor all the more those people who, living in conditions far worse than mine, have the courage to act with integrity and hope for the building of a better and more meaningful world, if only among people living close to them. They are acting in behalf of life and earth here and now, regardless of what they may believe or not believe about the hereafter. One of the all-time great lines in the Bible is Psalm 104, verse 33: "I will sing unto the Lord *as long as I live*; I will sing praise to my God *while I have my being* [emphasis mine]."

"As long as I live,... while I have my being" will I make such music as I am able, not waiting until I have been given a cloud to sit on and a harp to play. Grief makes it difficult to enter into the singing. But the courage to do so is the root and source of hope. Furthermore, such courage can seldom be engendered without the help of other people, without a chorus to sing in, without the realization that we are humanly involved, that we are not alone either in our joys or in our sorrows.

Literal meanings such as the truth of the law of gravity limit and condition our freedom in ways that we are foolish to ignore. Poetic meaning never forces, never compels us to conform; salvation is never guaranteed by a legend. Poetic meaning is quietly there as the deepest mode of persuasion, leaving us ever free to say yes or to deny. We are still stuck with our own freedom with respect to how we shall respond. Folklore, at best, is an encouragement, a means of inviting courage to come into our minds and bodies. Realized hope is the product of courageous action in concert with others of like courage. Those who worked in the 1960s for the cause of racial justice, in spite of their fears, generated among themselves the kind of hope nothing could discourage. The mothers of the disappeared who marched in the public square in Buenos Aires kept their hope alive by their simple, courageous, and corporate action against every lure of despair. So it is with many liberated folk in Central and South America, from Catholics to atheists, from Guatemala to Chile, whose fires of hope are fed by their acts of courage, whether or not those acts are also fueled by biblical folklore. I have no doubt that the hopes of Nelson Mandela were forged in imperishable steel by his minuscule actions within the tiny confines of his prison cell. When he walked out into the sunlight, he plunged directly into the hopeful actions of the thousands who welcomed him, especially the actions of that bright-eyed little robin of a prelate, the Archbishop Tutu. Hope is born among those who in concert with others seize the small or great possibilities of resurrection on any day of the world.

How many times did Norman Thomas run on the Socialist ticket for President of the United States? I don't remember. In any case, I am sure that he did not run because he hoped, much less expected, to win. He had hope precisely because he had the courage to run and others had the courage and willingness to help him run. Like those women who sat at the tomb under their paralyzing burden of grief, he and they responded to some kind of mysterious glory in their innermost selves and roused each other out of fear and dejection and ran full speed bearing good tidings. Religion should always be fraught with good tidings, should continually repeat the refrain "Be not afraid!" "Be of good cheer!" This is the encouragement of stories, the mystique of folklore, poetry, art, and music. Every folktale is best read as here and now, not simply as way back then.

I am tempted to rewrite a famous sentence attributed to St. Paul in his First Letter to the Corinthians: "Now abideth faith, hope, and love, these three. And the greatest of these is love." Sometimes, especially when I feel like a motherless child, I would prefer to say, without in any way denigrating love, "the greatest of these is hope." Hope is the metaphorical arrival of springtime to every "winter of discontent." How can we live without it?

Hope and the Holy Spirit

In my church and denomination, I have been dutifully trained to consider the Trinity as a kind of creative, symbolic representation, yet out-of-bounds for serious consideration. As a theologian I have been required to look at it dispassionately. And I have come to the conclusion that the Trinity was an invention not only of naïve wishful believers but also of sophisticates who needed some protection from their own tendencies toward skepticism or despair.

To some ancient philosophers, God, being changeless and immortally all-perfect, could not be tainted in the least by any material or human frailty. Such a God may attract human striving toward perfection, but would not be concerned about any degree of human success or failure. Such involvement might dilute the divine perfection. To the ancient Jewish rabbis and their Christian successors, God was not thought to be so beyond nature and humanity as to be remote, unapproachable, and beyond any effect, much less coercion from the natural world. From the early Jewish Christians came the astonishing claim that the great God, creator of heaven and earth, had allowed himself to be born into flesh, to be immersed in human ambiguity, in the human mess, be it illness, poverty, psychosis, family miseries, war, or bureaucratic helplessness. God came down to the human level, endured torture and martyrdom, returned to his own right hand, and promised, having felt at close range the frailty and savagery of earthly existence, to return one day and bring about a final salvation. Thus God was pictured as twofold, purely human and purely divine. God was the Eternal Creator and also the Revealed Messiah who had promised to return for the final redemption of the world.

Meanwhile, what encouragement did Christians receive for the intervening years of struggle prior to the Last Judgment? What hope that the earth is still the Kingdom of God, not the kingdom of the Devil? This hope of the final Kingdom of God, said the old-time Christians, is encouraged by the periodic experience of the visitation of the Holy Spirit, beginning with the sudden enlightenment of the apostles at Pentecost. God sends his Spirit hither and yon, as unexpectedly as the blowing of wind, unpredictable, now here, now there. In this respect, the Kingdom of God is already present and partially achieved.

These divine good deeds, however much hoped for, always seem to come as a surprise. They are believed to occur in the mystery of the Catholic Mass and the Protestant Communion. They can also occur in the artist's inspiration, the humble person's sudden gift of kindness, the radiance of a small child, and the gift of rain and coolness after drought. All these "saving" events can be interpreted as the infinite working and weaving of the Holy Spirit. In visual art such visitations are symbolized by tongues of flame or by the airborne arrival of a dove. Of course, such limited images point beyond their literal boundaries to the very mystery of God. What was twofold became threefold, and behold, the Trinity.

In modern liberal religious circles, it sometimes seems there is an implicit faith in the Holy Spirit, as though we are salvaging the "third person" of the Trinity from the disappearing first "two persons." The Holy Spirit is not unlike the lingering smile of a vanishing cosmic Cheshire Cat. Something there is in the goodness of humanity and in the never-failing ecological bounty of the natural world that will not be defeated. In the worst circumstances people and nature display not only cruelty or unconcern, but also unexpected kindness, bounty, and courage. During the Nazi occupation of Europe, those many gentiles who sheltered Jews at the risk of their lives are radiant instances of such a faith. Many non-Jews died for Jews and are now memorialized by living trees along the Avenue of the Righteous Gentiles in Jerusalem at Yad Vashem, the holocaust memorial. They were of the Holy Spirit. To put the words of Stephen Spender in a different context: "They traveled a short while towards the sun. And left the vivid air signed with their honor."

My first and continuing theological counsel to religious liberals is therefore not to get hung up on God the Father. Do not insist on affirming or denying the image of a supreme intelligent creator and director of the cosmos. Concentrate your wonder and your worship on what is near at hand, those beautiful and surprising irruptions of goodness and loveliness into the ordeals of a darkening humanity. Since all life moves unfailingly toward the dark of death, why not at least exult in the bright moments that are available every day of the journey?

We might move more easily to achieve this daily sparkle in the midst of failing light if it were not for a pressing commandment inherited from Christianity and more directly from Judaism: the human ethical responsibility to make the goodness prevail and to root out the evil. One must not merely relax in particular joys granted by the Holy Spirit. What we enjoy another person lacks. What we create may be at another person's expense. The very blessings of liberty and prosperity so freely given to our country are more often than not lacking in a hungry, polluted, and war-ravaged world. Also within our borders, one person's profits occur during another's unemployment. Joy and misery are intermingled, and only by a sacrifice of attention and compassion can we concentrate untroubled upon our own joys and good fortune.

Speaking theologically, the Holy Spirit seems to be curiously unthorough, unheeding, perhaps even irresponsible. It is not so omnipresent as God is supposed to be. It is blithely selective and ambiguous. The very cooling of a hot day may bring with it a tornado. Meanwhile every person is under the command to provide remedies to ills seemingly forgotten by the Holy Spirit.

The more I read the Hebrew Scriptures, the more I am impressed that the ancient Jews, quite without recourse to any Trinitarian doctrine, knew this inner tension between ethics and joy. They struggled with the image of the Creator who, in his great transcendence, seemed at times capricious to the verge of the unethical. Take, for example, the story of God encouraging the children of Israel to flee from Egypt while simultaneously encouraging the Egyptians to hold them in bondage by "hardening" Pharaoh's heart. Or the story of God who, in despair over the wickedness of humanity, created a major ecological disaster in the age of Noah for a world he had once considered "very good." The divine picture is sometimes savage, as in the command to Joshua and later to King Saul to destroy the enemy cities not only stone for stone, but down to the last living, man, woman, and child, and every piece of livestock.

The ancient narratives are extraordinarily candid in suggesting a less-than-perfect God, describing him as a "devouring fire," "mighty and terrible," the "God of battles" who works readily on the principle of "vengeance." Such honesty with respect to their own history also records instances in which mere human beings presume to give God ethical instructions. Of course this had to be done with extreme diplomacy, since the instructor is leading from weakness, not strength. In Genesis 18 when God announces his intention to destroy the wicked cities of Sodom and Gomorrah, Abraham worries about his relatives who live there. But instead of making a direct appeal for them in the name of self-interest, Abraham, negotiating with superb finesse, asks, "Will you indeed sweep away the righteous with the wicked? ... Far be it from you to do such a thing, to slay the righteous with the wicked, so that the righteous fare as the wicked! ... Shall not the Judge of all the earth do what is just?" (Genesis 18:23-25). Thus Abraham challenges the honor of God in bargaining for a reprieve until he can remove his family from danger—the first argument in world history against saturation bombing.

Moses also causes the Almighty to change his mind and thereby to admit tacitly that the Creator is something short of all-knowing. After the Israelite worship of the golden calf in Exodus 32, God threatens to destroy all the people and raise up a new righteous generation, with Moses as the sole surviving nucleus. Moses reacts with more practicality and ethical sensitivity, arguing that God's honor is suspect if he does not rescue his chosen ones. He also asks God rhetorically whether he intends to keep his promises made long ago to Abraham, Isaac, and Jacob. "And the Lord changed his mind about the disaster that he had planned to bring on his people" (Exodus 32:14). Thus the ancient Israelites believed that the caprice of the Almighty can, on occasion, be bent into a humble reversal of divine policy by human appeal, using God's own ethics.

One does not have to look far for the social and political source of Jewish theological ambiguity about the nature of God. From the beginning their yearning for a stable and honorable civilization took the form of the dream of a promised land delivered to them by the action of a divine power and authority. This dream was for a little land, but rich in resources; a modest land, yet powerful in defense and in divine authority; an unaggressive land, yet one where they could live and respect themselves without danger of invasion. This dream may have been briefly and partially fulfilled in the one brief period of the monarchies of Kings Saul, David, and Solomon from about 1000 BCE until 922 AD. Then it fell apart into two kingdoms. One of these kingdoms was conquered by the Assyrians, the second by Babylonia. A tiny replica was restored under Nehemiah a century and a half later, only to be overrun by Alexander the Great. Egyptian control supervened, followed by Syrian control. For a brief hundred years the Maccabean revolt set up a semi-autonomous Jewish kingdom, which the

Romans eventually wiped out. From 70 CE until 1948 the dream of an Israelite nation was lost. Meanwhile, the people, scattered over the world, were subjected to an unending series of humiliations, indignities, and atrocities. During all that time Jews had to remind a capricious God or fate of their eternal covenant: a prosperous and peaceful life in return for human righteousness.

During this millennial struggle, Jewish successes in the creation of civilization and personal well-being are remarkable despite their miserable history. All their history points to the main outlines of their theology, which are these: (1) God demands righteousness even when it hurts and does not make practical sense; (2) humanity demands some kind of reward for righteousness, which is to say, the relation between Creator and creature is contractual, a covenant; (3) both parties to the covenant periodically fail—from time to time the wicked flourish, the righteous suffer, God appears wicked or unconcerned rather than righteous; (4) yet, for all that, ethics does not lose relevance. The Jewish people survive. Not only do they survive, they survive to be eminently creative as minorities in cultures worldwide.

It is my contention that Christians, undergoing some of the same evil hazards and happy surprises as their fellow Jews, tended to assign these uncertainties to the suffering of Christ or the absence of the Holy Spirit, they being too pious to add these frailties to the nature and responsibility of the single unity of one God. The Christians regarded God the Father as too good to be ambiguous. The Jews had no need for the Christians' elaborate three-way division of divine labor. God is necessarily ambiguous by virtue of his close involvement in human history. Conversely, human history written large is sacred, sacred in its sufferings as well as in its triumphs. The Creator is involved in the ambiguities of the creatures. Thus the ambiguities of earth are not wholly without sacred dimensions. Even as the Creator is never ultimately defeated, so the creature should try not to commit the ultimate sin of despair. One must continue to hope and to praise, even from the Warsaw

Ghetto, even from the death camps. What Christians saw in the one and only death and resurrection of Jesus Christ, Jews have seen everywhere: the deaths of dear ones, dear places, and dear hopes. And beyond these, the New Life, here, and everywhere. When Jesus was reported to have risen from the dead, he inadvertently created a new religion. When the Jewish remnants of Europe rose from the ashes of the death camps, they created a new nation. They did it by prayer and by action. They doggedly insisted in prayer that their God honor the ancient covenant. And they courageously struggled against a mountain of contrary evidence and desperate antagonists to do what was seemingly impossible: to establish, a few years after their greatest ordeal, a free and independent nation. They illustrate the truth of the Christian Epistle of James in the New Testament: "For just as the body without the spirit is dead, so faith without works is also dead" (James 2:26).

James speaks of the spirit. I think we may safely say that what gives a human being the energy to overcome the seemingly impossible is that inexplicable margin of spiritual trust in the goodness of life, which is not of our making. In the language of an old hymn, Spirit, the Holy Spirit is that "love which will not let us go" even though from time to time it appears to let us down.

The sacredness of Spirit—which is at least the human spirit, which I would prefer to call the World Spirit or Holy Spirit since I do not believe that the human species has a monopoly on it—the sacredness of spirit is essentially free from guile. It appears to achieve greatness without those nasty calculations and piracies by which the merely powerful rise to power. Spirit is the greatness in Mozart in the midst of his personal miseries, not the greatness of Hitler in the midst of his self-aggrandizing triumphs. Spirit is the greatness of Abraham Lincoln at the center of his deep personal sadness, not the notoriety of Richard Nixon engulfed by his own endless scheming and trickery. Spirit is that muscular goodness that Jesus speaks of as "wise as serpents and innocent as doves" (Matthew 10:16), that schemes in righteousness for the sake of a righteous nation, that perseveres against the dinosaurs of the merely powerful and does so not out of hatred for evil persons but out of love for all people and the real and hoped-for righteousness of their communion and communities. Spirit never fools itself into thinking that the good life is automatic, easy, to be had without sacrifice or secured without constant watchfulness. Spirit never relaxes long in despair, letting the evil flow into the vacuum of its own inattention and abandoned guardianship.

In the biblical literature you will find such tragedy as will make your own yoke seem easy and your burden light. There you will find a symphony of nature and humanity in which tragedy is perpetually overcome by new creation, new being, new hope. You can call it nature and humanity; you can call it Jehovah and his world and people; you can call it Father, Son, and Holy Spirit; you can call it none of these and devise your own names. Your own linguistic choice will not cause a single one of the ancient characters of the Bible to so much as twitch in their graves. But the richness, the scope of tragedy and triumph, despair and hope, are all with us. They are not there to be simply exalted in their ancient language. They are there to stimulate new words and new language by their perennial wisdom and encouragement.

We should not assume that all committed Christians are rigid and uninventive with respect to their own tradition. I think of a mature man, the father of many children, a craftsman of consummate skill working tirelessly and patiently with mediocre helpers; a man who never lost his vision despite the loss of beloved children, cherished positions, and high ambitions. He so loved people and the world and the excruciating exactions of his art that he died not quite completing a supreme masterpiece while lying on his deathbed. He called to his bedside an old friend and dictated to him a simple choral prelude on the old Lutheran hymn "Before Thy Throne I Now Ascend." I like to think that in those last hours, Johann Sebastian Bach may have recited to himself, with just a hint of his own music for it, a small part of his greatest masterpiece, the *Mass in B Minor*. The text I have in mind, with the beginning word "Credo" or "I believe," reads: "Et in unum spiritum sanctum Dominum et vivificantem"—"And in the Holy Spirit, the Lord and life-giving one."

Vivificantem—a beautiful word: giving life, creating life, life-making, life-fostering, life-nurturing, life-celebrating. This part of Bach's *Mass*, a bass solo, occurs in the midst of the huge center section of the work, the Credo or Nicene Creed. Much of that creed, which is not biblical, is not congenial to religious liberals. But its human and musical drama is universal, and never more than when Bach's musical line soars into the realm of the Holy Spirit. What else can create any kind of worldwide community of faith except a mysterious spirit that humanly and naturally abides amid all human and natural differences, that humanly and naturally triumphs amid all human and natural miseries, that ties into one ecological family all the living creatures of this most cherished and fragile planet?

Divine Justice in the Hebrew Bible

THERE ARE MANY ANSWERS to the question "Why do bad things happen to good people?" For instance, some good people, by reason of their innocence of evil, can sometimes be deceived and swindled. Good people, especially children, can be careless and fail to notice how thin the ice is where they are playing. Good people are occasionally too proud of their supposed goodness and estrange themselves from others by their excessive moralism. Or the most compelling explanation: Good people tend to challenge the status quo, thereby making enemies of those who defend and profit by the status quo. In this category we find Jesus, Lincoln, Gandhi, Martin Luther King, and many lesser luminaries. The people of Jewish ancestry and loyalty have understood this dynamic for millennia. They have lived by strong moral codes and have challenged business as usual. Also, by age-long habits of personal discipline, they have excelled in many fields of human endeavor. Their goodness and their excellence have aroused envy and created enemies. This has gone on so long that Jews have invented the sardonic slogan "No good deed goes unpunished." Of one thing we may be sure: Many who suffer some kind of catastrophe are tempted to ask, "Why did this happen to me?" The implication is that they are worthy of a better fate. Or like the would-be comforters of Job, they believe that God awards each person his or her just dues.

Back of this doctrine of the absolute justice of God is the tradition that God is omnipotent and omniscient, embodying the kind of power that we in our finitude will never reach. God is alleged to know absolutely every event the future carries and able to fulfill his foreknown future down to the last syllable. And his goodness being without flaw, the scenario of all events in time is of equal value. This image of God's perfection is a classical rather than a biblical heritage. It comes from Plato and his successors who dreamed of an ideal perfection immortally existing without any shadow of change. Human suffering is a consequence of the imperfections of the material world, not the responsibility of the divine perfection.

The Hebrew Bible, in those traditions not yet influenced by classical philosophical standards, does not dream of such a God. One may read their theological attitudes quite plainly in their myths of interaction between God and his people. In sum, God both orders judgment and discovers a need to bypass judgment and show mercy. He is mighty beyond all other powers, but not almighty. He can be influenced to reverse his own will. He is wise but not omniscient, in the sense that he must wait for persons to act before he can decide how to react.

God must punish Adam and Eve in some way for their disobedience. But, as the myth makes clear, he cannot write them off completely. He launches them out of the protections of Eden and into the outside world, armed with their newfound knowledge of good and evil. He sees how they are already suffering shame after the Fall and will suffer more. He evidently knows that the knowledge of their own nakedness has injured them psychologically; he knows that they need clothing to protect them from shame and from the weather. So even as he expels them from Eden, "And the Lord made garments of skins for the man and for his wife, and clothed them" (Genesis 3:21), thereby protecting both their mental and physical health.

That is not all. Much worse causes of judgment and stronger needs for mercy follow in the mythology of Genesis. Cain, firstborn of Adam and Eve, commits first-degree murder against his brother, Abel. And the murderer has the nerve to plead, "Am I my brother's keeper?" (Genesis 4:9). If the same circumstance happened today between two brothers, the survivor would get either capital punishment or life imprisonment. Instead, in the biblical story Cain is exiled, not from life, but from God's presence. To the ancient Jews, that exile into the wilderness east of Eden is comparable to a death sentence. Cain knows this and wails that anyone who finds him will be free to kill him. So God puts a special mark on him that means, "Whoever kills Cain will suffer a sevenfold vengeance" (Genesis 4:15). This principle nicely matches the provision in our Constitution that no one can be punished twice for the same crime. Furthermore, Genesis 4 tells how Cain's descendants become heroic inventors of civilization: One builds a city; one invents tents and shepherding; one is the ancestor of all who make music, thus giving birth to the arts; and a fourth discovers how to smelt metals and fashion tools of bronze and iron, the first industrial revolution. The sins of the fathers and mothers are not visited even upon those who "went out from the presence of the Lord." The ungodly descendants of a brother-killer are allowed to flourish.

As the Genesis myths unfold, God's exasperation with humanity comes close to total cynicism. In Genesis 9, the Lord finds humanity so evil that he wants to destroy not only the human race but the whole of creation (except the fish) by bringing a colossal flood on the earth. Fortunately for humanity and the rest of nature, the myth goes on to say that God's cynical exasperation does not include Noah and his family or the other living species on earth. Noah "found favor" in God's eyes and is given explicit directions for building a saving ark, with the command to include one pair each of all living species to accompany his voyage on the great flood. What is most human and humane about the Noah legend is the picture of God's repentance for the flood and for the destruction of most of the

creation he once valued as "very good." He promises Noah he will
never again do such a thing, and being somewhat forgetful in his advanced age, God puts the rainbow in the sky to remind himself as
well as Noah and his descendants that never again will there be total
destruction of the beautiful orders of earthly nature.

These "images of God" plus others previously mentioned are
preeminently parental. A loving parent uses punishment as little
as possible and is always ready to show mercy. Children are not
free to do whatever they please. If a parent does not restrain them,
society or various natural consequences surely will bring restraints, which are often more brutal and destructive than what
the parent would have delivered. This is a world where freedom is
real and consequences are real. The child, however disobedient,
must eventually be free of the parent's total domination. In the
case of Adam and Eve, God's prohibition of the fruit of the tree of
knowledge does not compromise their freedom to come to maturity and thereby to experience good and evil. In the case of Cain,
his descendants find a rightful place in the world. In the case of
Noah, God repents his initial angry judgment against humanity
and makes it possible for a universal healing to take place.

One way to read these early Hebrew legends is to see in them
a realistic picture of the nature of human history. A nonmechani-
cal system of human behavior is certain to contain conflict and
degeneration from the original goodness of divine creation.
Freedom granted to those created "in God's image" means an inevitable possibility of damage to the human-divine image. Such a
development makes both judgment and mercy equally necessary.
The Hebrew divine-human drama is not about perfect order and
security; it includes elements of struggle, fall, repentance, and renewal in the earth as it is, not as existence might be in some distant, static, and perfect heavenly kingdom.

This paradoxical picture of human life on earth—of human and
natural interactions that are sometimes beautiful and good, sometimes ugly and evil, no matter what we plan or wish—is the ultimate

reason why bad things happen to good people, why good things happen to bad people, why good things happen to good people, and why bad things happen to bad people. What we call chance in nature and freedom in human nature is as universal as any causality and predictability, whether natural, or divine, or both. One must question the doctrine of the omnipotence of God, as well as the opinion that God is completely good according to human standards.

All of these questions about the justice of God are raised in the Book of Job. The prologue to Job's long poem of suffering and lamentation shows a picture of God willing to risk his own reputation for righteousness by a wager with Satan. God has boasted to Satan of Job's righteousness. Satan replies that Job finds it easy to be righteous because he has everything he needs. Take away his property, his children, and his health, and Job will easily curse God. God presumes to allow Satan to torment Job in order to prove that no amount of deprivation or suffering will shake Job's faith and allegiance to his maker. Satan performs all his tortures on Job, but Job's response is different from what either God or Satan has predicted. God is right in that Job does not curse God as even Job's wife urges him to do. Satan is right because Job will not accept his suffering as just.

Everyone who has read the Book of Job knows how he is visited by three "comforters" who presume to explain Job's suffering as divine punishment for unknown or unremembered sins. Job maintains his essential righteousness, and without cursing God, he curses his own life and wishes only for the comfort of death. This irresolvable argument proceeding for many pages, the three friends finally leave Job to suffer and grieve alone.

Then God's voice comes to Job out of a whirlwind. It is a powerful defense of the idea that neither Job nor any human being begins to understand the majesty and mystery of all of creation, that what God does cannot be challenged as just or unjust, given the weakness of human understanding. Job is properly humbled and admits that his challenges to God's justice are meaningless. His reply to God's thunderous voice ends with these somber words:

> I had heard of you by the hearing of the ear, but now my eye sees you; therefore I despise myself, and repent in dust and ashes.
>
> —Job 42:5-6

It would appear that Job is agreeing with his would-be comforters, that God's treatment of him is a just recompense for his sins. Contrariwise, it seems to me that if Job is really repentant, one must conclude that God is a self-centered tyrant who is willing to play dice with the devil in order to secure his reputation. However, in Jack Miles's *God: A Biography*, he translates the above passage as follows:

> Word of you has reached my ears, but now that my eyes have seen you, I shudder for sorrow for mortal clay.

This translation could be further interpreted as follows: "God, I have heard all kinds of nice things about you, but now I see exactly what you are. Therefore there is no point in my making any arguments about my own worthiness. Like a common worm, I now despise my own human hopes and former religious values. You have completely reduced me to that combination of dust and ashes that death will eventually make of me."

Whatever the original author meant to convey, God was evidently stung by Job's final word. Consider the very next verses, where God speaks to one of the three comforters, Eliphaz the Temanite:

> My wrath is kindled against you and against your two friends; for you have not spoken of me what is right, as my servant Job has. Now therefore take seven bulls and seven rams and go to my servant Job, and offer up for yourselves a burnt offering; and my servant Job shall pray for you, for I will accept his prayer not to deal with you according to your folly; for you have not spoken of me what is right, as my servant Job has done.
>
> —Job 42:7-8

In genuine fear for themselves, the three comforters do exactly as they are bidden, including sending an invitation to Job to attend their expiatory service. And three verses later, the text reads:

And the Lord restored the fortunes of Job when he had prayed for his friends; and the Lord gave Job twice as much as he had before.

—Job 42:10

The book ends thus:

After this Job lived one hundred and forty years, and saw his children, and his children's children, four generations. And Job died, old and full of days.

—Job 42:17

Most scholars believe that this concluding episode is a later priestly addition to the great poetry of Job's humiliations. I do not have the scholarship to measure the accuracy of this theory. However, from a literary point of view, this final chapter of the Book of Job opens up several plausible dramatic reasons for its having been included in the canon.

The divine restitution of Job's family and fortune accords with the constant pattern in Hebrew legend where God reacts to the people's needs and sins appropriately rather than foreknowing and dictating their history in advance. As already indicated, he shows mercy as well as judgment to Adam and Eve; he does not slay Cain as punishment for murder, but protects his future and allows his descendants to flourish; and he repents of the damages caused by the great flood and secures the future of creation by favoring Noah, as well as promising to protect all generations from any total world disaster. There are many other instances of the divine flexibility exercised in response to unforeseen events. God does not carry through his original command to Abraham to slay his own son; he changes his mind about his proposed destruction of Sodom and Gomorrah after Abraham argues against it; he blesses Jacob after Jacob challenges him (or his divine agent) in mortal combat; he allows the family of Jacob to flourish despite the serious sins of Jacob's older sons in selling their brother Joseph into slavery; he repents from his threat to destroy the refugees from Egypt for their worship of the golden calf, this in response to Moses' passionate plea for his mercy; he permits David to become the corner-stone of the Jerusalem monarchy despite David's sins of murder and adultery; and through all the ages of the prophets, he keeps alive the covenant in spite of the many times the people stray from its provisions. This pattern of a less-than-omnipotent deity acting in response to genuine human needs is dramatically repeated in his recognition of Job's legitimate charges against him. Job wins his case; the "comforters" lose theirs.

The actual means of Job's recovery from grief, illness, and despair are of great interest. The Bible claims no miracle in this regard. All God does is command the comforters to hold a religious service and to sacrifice for their misleading and false arguments against Job's misery, with the added command that they invite Job to the service. Job then displays his magnanimity by coming back into the community from his grief-stricken isolation to join in prayers for the very trio that had rubbed so much salt into his wounds. Although the story says that the Lord changed the fortunes of Job "after he prayed for his friends," the actual restoration details are given by the community. They take up a large collection of gold and give it to Job, by means of which Job is able to rebuild his economic position eventually into a condition of great wealth.

I find a psychological truth in these details. When a person is in profound grief, he or she becomes inaccessible. Not just the comforters, but the whole community is forced to abandon him or her and go on with their own lives. Job, however much he has argued with his friends, still considers them his friends, at least to the extent of rousing himself from his paralytic grief and attending their service and even going so far as to pray for them. Most people in Job's position would not have stirred a foot in that direction. Once Job put himself back into the heart of the community, his many friends saw some hope for his restoration and began immediately to provide the means for it.

If the honor of God is in any jeopardy in the entire Job story, it is in the prologue, where Job's suffering is the direct result of a chance wager between God and Satan. But the restoration of God's honor is not without precedent, as witnessed by the many stories of divine flexibility with respect to a balance of judgment and mercy.

I see yet another way of looking at the Book of Job that might reduce altogether the need to save God's honor by the means used in Job's last chapter. This has to do with one's interpretation of chapters 38 through 41, God's direct answer "out of the whirlwind" to Job's lamentations. These chapters precede the book's final chapter, describing Job's restoration.

This long and powerful burst of poetry begins with the challenge "Who is this that darkens counsel with words without knowledge?" What does Job know about the creation of the world, the establishment of the lights of heaven, the arrangement of the seas and dry lands? What does he understand about death and the abyss of darkness? Can he control the lions hunting their prey? Does he give scavengers their corpses to feed upon? Does he control floods or lightning? Is it by Job's wisdom that the valor of the horse rages in the midst of battles, that the hawk or eagle seeks its prey from on high and exults in killing to feed its young? "Can you draw out Leviathan with a fishhook, or press down its tongue with a cord? . . . Will it make many supplications to you? Will it speak soft words to you? Will it make a covenant with you to be taken as your servant forever?" (Job 41:1-4).

All these rhetorical questions do not describe creation as "very good" from a purely human standpoint. Here we find a recognition of the powers, to us sometimes benign and often savage, in the natural world, a world in which the creatures are destined to feed upon one another, where death is just as much a means to life as birth is. Here is a picture of nature, the cruelties of which have often been used to deny any action or presence of a loving deity. Nature "red in tooth and claw" is not usually the recipient of prayer. God seems to be asking Job, Why should your puny disasters be considered exceptional or worthy of blame?

From a contemporary point of view, there is a certain ecological justice expressed in the "voice out of the whirlwind." The creatures mentioned in these powerful passages are not there solely or at all for the purpose of human exploitation. In Henry Beston's words from *The Outermost House*:

> The animals shall not be measured by man. In a world older and more complete than ours, they move finished and complete, gifted with extensions of the senses we have lost or never attained, living by voices we shall never hear. They are not brethren, they are not underlings, they are other nations caught with ourselves in the net of life and time, fellow prisoners of the splendor and travail of the earth.

Job is being told that the sources of his pain are the consequences of orders of reality that have done nothing other than what they were made to do and are accustomed to do. They are not established to be governed by a human scale of rectitude. Bad things happen to good and to bad people not because of human virtue or wickedness, but because the world lives, ebbs, and flows by a combination of vitalities and pains largely beyond human control. This is as much as saying that God's wager with Satan, giving Satan the power to oppress Job, is backed up by the very nature of reality from the beginning.

I think it is remarkable that the Hebrew Scriptures should have achieved this level of realism, despite their predominant emphasis on the correlation of human righteousness and human prosperity. How different from the foregoing argument are the provisions of Moses' final sermons to the people of Israel just before his death:

> Therefore keep the commandments of the Lord your God, by walking in his ways and by fearing him. For the Lord your God is bringing you into a good land, a land with flowing streams, with springs and underground waters welling up in valleys and hills; a land of wheat and barley, of vines and fig trees and pomegranates, a land of olive trees and honey; a land where you may eat bread without scarcity, where you will lack nothing, a land whose

stones are iron and from whose hills you may mine copper. You shall eat your fill and bless the Lord your God for the good land that he has given you. Take care that you do not forget the Lord your God, by failing to keep his commandments, his ordinances, and his statues, which I am commanding you today.

—Deuteronomy 8:6-11

Israel often had reason to suspect the validity of their covenant with God to receive prosperity in exchange for obedience. They often asked such questions as "How long, O Lord, will the land mourn and the grass of every field wither?" (Jeremiah 12:4). I find it remarkable that the possibility of understanding divine justice differently should be found in such a powerful portion of the Bible as the Book of Job.

There is yet another place in the Hebrew Scriptures where we find a kind of reconciliation between faith in God's rewards for righteousness and the recognition that divine sovereignty extends in realms beyond humanity and that this broader sense of divine authority is itself a matter of glory rather than dismay. I refer to Psalm 104, a long poem that contains these words:

Thou make darkness, and it is night, where all the animals of the forest come creeping out. The young lions roar for their prey, seeking their food from God. When the sun rises, they withdraw and lie down in their dens. People go out to their work and to their labor until the evening. O Lord, how manifold are your works! In wisdom you have made them all; the earth is full of your creatures. Yonder is the sea, great and wide, creeping things innumerable are there, living things both small and great. There go the ships, and Leviathan that you formed to sport in it. These all look to you to give them their food in due season; when you give to them, they gather it up; when you open your hand, they are filled with good things. When you hide your face, they are dismayed; when you take away their breath, they die and return to their dust. When you send forth your spirit, they are created; and you renew the face of the ground.... I will sing to the Lord as long as I live; I will sing praise to my God while I have my being.

—Psalm 104:20-30, 33

Here is a celebration of the natural world and its natural functions without regard to any favoritism on God's part for any human group or for humanity as a whole.

Myths and mythological symbols are always fluid and should never be treated as possessing one inevitable meaning. The ancient Jews understood this in collecting various interpretations of Scripture in the Talmud, interpretations that were often conflicting and sometimes contradictory. Out of deference to the ultimate mystery of the divine and the finite nature of human understanding, they preserved in the Talmud a kind of intellectual economy of abundance rather than reduce the meanings of Scripture to exclusive dogmas.

Any free church can do no less. The biblical treasury exists to stimulate religious thought and opinion, not to tie it down in rigid dogmas. There is something comforting about realizing that issues that hurt and challenge us today have an ancient history among members of the human species long since dead. Others have discovered that life can be painful and unfair and at the same time worth living and cherishing. In sharing their assurances, we strengthen our own.

Through the Rose Window

THE ROSE WINDOW of the First Unitarian Church of Chicago has fascinated me ever since I first saw it in 1943. Designed and made by Charles Connick of Boston, one of America's most respected stained-glass makers, it is rightly scaled to the proportions of the church building: brilliant and yet simple, dramatic, yet unpretentious. The architect of the church, Denison Hull, told me that Connick designed the window to represent archangels, with the feeling that such a theme might be appropriate to a Unitarian church. Much contemplation has assured me that the theme is appropriate, even though we have no record of why Connick thought so.

The circle of the window is divided into four trefoils, or clover-like triangles. Between the upper corners of each trefoil is a small wedge that contains a human face. Originally I thought these might be the four Gospel writers or perhaps they are unnamed people serving to represent you and me, causing us to feel that we are involved in the window, looking out of it and not simply looking at it from afar. On closer look I saw that each of these small figures had red wings and androgynous faces, neither male nor female. These details establish each of them as angels. Furthermore, their small size and relatively simple undifferentiated features seemed to elevate the four larger angels of the trefoils to the status of archangels, thereby confirming the character Connick had assigned them.

The North Angel is the only one who is standing and whose wings are spread as though ready for flight. It holds a sword point down at parade rest, in a position of guardianship rather than aggression. To me this is a symbol of benign government, of the human necessity to govern and be governed by law rather than by arbitrary force. There is no viable society without custom and courtesy, including large portions of its custom and courtesy codified into law. And there is no law without some kind of police authority to enforce it. We individualists who pride ourselves on being free spirits could not survive without some degree of conformity, most of it willing conformity, in order to give human life some viable order and structure. The North Angel appears to me as the Angel of Law and Order.

While granting these truths about the functions of government and law, we would be most uncomfortable if the North Angel were the only presence in our window. Our deeper and more natural inclinations, especially since this church stands in the neighborhood of the University of Chicago, gravitate to the South Angel, whom I shall call the Angel of the Book. It sits quietly and openly, an open book in its lap, its arms spread and its gaze outward-bound. We see a picture of mental observation, of study and writing, and in the open gesturing hands, an image of eloquence—all hallmarks of the thinker and teacher. Its task requires a sedentary location. It depends wholly on the North Angel for protection. The Angel of the Book needs privacy, quiet, and the opportunity for contemplation, for reasoning, writing, and free interchange with fellow scholars—all necessary ingredients of learning and scholarship. Unless such guardianship of free thought and free scholarship is maintained, there is likelihood that the raw power of the North Angel, the Angel of Law and Order, will degenerate into tyranny.

If such degeneration occurs, the Thinker's Angel of the Book is helpless. In the worst of situations, the Thinker's only recourse is self-censorship or martyrdom.

These considerations suggest that democratic law depends upon a respect for law created by the participation of an educated citizenry. The two angels, the Angel of Law and Order and the Angel of the Book, are guardians of human civilization. They also form the main axis of our free religious culture, just as they form the main axis of our window. The only just and moral reason for unsheathing a lethal weapon is to guard the freedom of action and thought among law-abiding people. To be savage is to reject the fruits of the mind or to corrupt them and use them for the spoliation of life. When each end of the axis respects the other, the better angels of our nature, like the glorious angels of our window, stand in lovely symmetrical balance—in a mutual solicitude. Then we and they are mutually fulfulfilled. In many ways the history of liberal religion has been the effort to educate people to harmonize the functions of the North and South Angels. We have always professed to love knowledge, science, and wisdom from all parts of the earth. We have always professed to love the state, to cherish the social good, and to work for the betterment of humanity in our common life.

However, for me religion involves something more than book learning and social action. And a glance at our beautiful window and the West and East angels will tell us what that something more is. In contrast to the upright positions of the axial angels, everything about the lateral angels is oblique. Their bodies are turned partly toward and partly away from us; the lines of their anatomies make a diagonal zigzag; even the base lines on which they rest are tilted slightly off the horizontal. There is in them a transcendence of all that is rigid, frontal, and merely rectilinear.

The West Angel is a musician, its instrument a trumpet. Consider the particular virtues of the trumpet. It can sound a call to action, or it can be a soothing nocturnal benediction playing taps. It is both powerful and gentle. By extension this angel is any and every artist, not only the giants of fine arts who appear in our museums, concert halls, theaters and libraries, but every professional or amateur who loves the beauty and vitality of the arts and who is willing to spend time working in or enjoying one or more artistic realm. Human beings were involved in artistic activities long before they learned logic or science. It is quite conceivable that religion and the arts grew from the same root. Artistic expressions of the beauty and magnificence of human experience lead to proclamations of celebration and praise. Artistic representations of grief and sorrow create the mode of petitionary prayer, along with gestures in ritual form to mollify the enemy and the demon—in each case to show forth a mystical healing power restoring body and soul.

It is the task of all the arts to signify and amplify human values and powers whether in a mood of celebration or in an elegaic expression of grief and suffering. See how the Angel of the Book inclines its head toward the trumpet, as if it is touched by some influence speaking in a new key, leading it to a recognition of human values beyond the details of everyday phenomena. Let us also not fail to notice that the trumpet of the West Angel is a ram's horn trumpet, symbolizing the Jewish call to repentance on Yom Kippur. This is a call that all persons need to hear, especially those among us who are most proud and self-assured.

The East Angel cradles a shepherd's crook in one hand and arm, suggesting the pastor, or overseer of a flock of sheep, one who feeds, shelters, and guards the general welfare of the flock. This role of Caretaker Angel also points beyond the role of pastor to all the other helping functions of human society within and beyond the need for food, clothing, and shelter. The Caretaker Angel's other hand holds a jar upright, suggesting a container—for seeds, water or wine, medicine, flowers, or all sorts of goods for economic use and well-being. The East Angel, the Good Shepherd, combines all those economic and helping functions by which a people is able to live and to live well. It reminds us that much of the function of community is not based primarily on learning or governmental power, but on the basic trust and generosity of service among people of every degree of sophistication or naïveté. The kind word, the compassionate act, the tender loving care—whether in the family, the neighborhood, a professional agency, or even the generosity of a stranger—keep our world essentially a place of home rather than a wasteland. In fact, too much professionalism in this realm of helping the needy may erode the sympathy we should learn as infants from our parents and pass on to others in our maturity.

Notice how the South Angel below inclines its head toward the West Angel, the Angel of Artistry. There is little scholarship that can make its way into public opinion for the general welfare unless it is somehow creatively expressed. The scholar must reach toward the eloquence that music embodies. Words must not only be spoken; they must be sung, or at least spoken or written lyrically. In public singing we have a vehicle by which ideas work their way into action. In poetic expression we touch the mind and heart simultaneously. Without the dimension of artistry, the mere management of affairs loses insight into the subtleties of human joy and human need.

Socrates argued that virtue or, in better translation, excellence is knowledge. He was martyred for his beliefs, and there was no Angel of Law and Order to save his life from popular fear and hatred. His dream of the Philosopher-King is like our hope that knowledge will lead to individual goodness and good legislation and that the combination of these two goods will guarantee a good society. Unlike Socrates, we must face the reality that power tends to corrupt even philosophers, that the powers of government are not guaranteed to be pure because they are brilliant.

Imagine the Rose Window with only two triangles, north and south, each balanced on the apex of the other. So fragile a form would be unnerving to look at and irrational as a symbol of the source of our personal and communal hopes. We cannot hope even to be civilized, not to mention protected in serenity and peace of mind, if we depend purely on learning and legislation. Two such impossibly balanced triangles would collapse.

Only when the North and South Angels are laterally buttressed by the horizontal triangles of the East and West angels is the knowledge-power axis made firm and upright. What protects their lovely poise are the two lateral triangles, buffering the precarious balance of the swordsman's pride and joining him, by the grace of the full circle, with the bookman's meditation. Here there is no falling, only the mystery of music and the arts inspiring thought while tempering any tendency in knowledge to become fanatical. Sympathy, healing, and forgiveness encourage the weak to become strong and the conscience of the strong to be sensitive toward human fallibility and suffering. Here there is no falling, only turning, as first our courage, then our music, then our thoughtful reflection, then our sympathies can be uppermost.

If my idealism for our window's effect and influence seems excessive, you may be sure that my hope for the human future is tempered by anxieties common to us all. However, I have a long-term optimism toward the survival and growth of civilization symbolized in a few aspects of our window not yet discussed. Notice that each of the three angels East, South, and West has a tongue of flame on its head, while the North Angel does not. To me this says that human and divine love, human and divine truth, and human and divine beauty all belong in the primal creativity of our world. This spiritual fire can enter and transcend every finite location and local situation. No local catastrophe is ultimate for these realities. By contrast the North Angel, Guardian of Law and Order, has no such flame on its head. Its power derives from beyond itself, from the other three archangels. Its authority exists only as derived from the other three.

My other cause for confidence in the power of our window is more mystical because it is derived not from the window's explicit symbolism or geometry, but rather from the window's colors. Red—the color of fire, the color of blood—is the color of courage. It speaks of the life that does not fear to blossom and be strong. The life-sustaining fluid within us, revealed in the flushes of our excitements or shed in the moment of ordeal and sacrifice, has its blazing reflection in our window. Gold—the color of precious metal and the color of the sun—is the color of wisdom and glory. It speaks of that great heart of life ninety-three million miles away that has given us our earth and kept the earth replenished with plant life through the wonderful chemistry of chlorophyll and sugar. We are warmed externally by the sun, internally by the products of the sun. Green—the color of grasses, stems, and the leaves in the forested plains and mountains of the world—is the principal banner of our life-sustaining earth. As the color of spring, green points to the mystery of renewal. As the color of plant life, green represents the triumph of seeds buried in the dark earth. Blue—the color of the sky and the color of water—is the most mystical color of all. It combines the heights of heaven and the depths of the sea. It is a radiant sunlit hue, but it speaks also of the cool of evening and peacefulness in the human heart. There is the sparkle of blue eyes. There is even blue at midnight. And in the windows of Chartres cathedral in France is the most marvelous blue of all—a blue so rich, so bright, so gentle, and so comforting to me—that above all color that I have ever seen anywhere in the world by day or in my dreams by night, it speaks to me of the blessing of God. From Chartres I return to our own church and see the blue of its windows with new eyes.

The time will come when you and I will be beyond the clear memory and ministrations of our Rose Window angels. We shall grow weary of our books, and we shall no longer worry whether the sword is raised against us or in our protection. We shall be beyond all earthly help. We shall be very much alone unless we are blessed to carry within us, at least up to the gates of death, the memory of colors—the red, the gold, the green, and especially the blue. I may not be able to remember the forms or functions of our angels, but I would like to remember the quality of the light that shone through them.

The invention of stained glass has both a factual and symbolic effect. In the factual sense, the glass polarizes the white, all-blinding, pure light into its constituent colors. In the symbolic sense, the stained glass helps us to intuit the many-colored meanings possible within our background of mystery. The human inventions and fashionings of art and myth, like the natural filters of sunlight, make it possible for us to sing the reality of the divine, although without precise or complete understanding. There would be no human religion without converting the superhuman divinity into humanoid stories. Similarly there would be no art without converting the outward forms of nature (including human nature) into human artifacts. By such labors the depths of life become an alternation of humility and awe, of mystery and meaning. In the end we can make no claim to perfection. In the end I pray that we may be privileged to feel and express the bliss of gratitude.

PRAYERS

Prayer for the Earth

Blessed art thou, Creator, Sustainer, and Renewer of this lovely planet wherein we have our home and our hope. All creatures, even in their strangeness, are akin to us, living by the same light and air and water, nourished by the same nutrients. In our deeds and choices, their lives as well as our own are held in the balance.

Thou has given us dominion over the earth, yet we have used our power to destroy life, not to affirm it. Grant us the wisdom to live by letting live, the forbearance to restrain our greed among the great abundances of creation, the gentleness to respect the gift of life by seeking to preserve it wherever we are able.

We ask these powers, O Lord, not for ourselves alone, but for our children's children and for all those living things that will seek to flourish beyond our deaths. Bless thou the earth and let thy redeeming love remain to preserve it forever and ever. *Amen.*

Prayer for the Sacred Community

O thou nameless one, center and soul of every happening, yet
more distant than the farthest star and more unknown, we cry
unto thee across light-years; we whisper unto thee from our own
breath and heart.

Abide within our darkness that we may praise thee in the light.
Let the human face, the human touch, the human love of all
things good and fair not forsake us. Bind us into the community
of the caring, and make us strong to care even though we are
weak and destined to die. Bind us into the community of all
sacred listeners who, beyond the silence of their own mortality,
have heard notes, and phrases, and tunes of thine own immortal
music. *Amen.*

Blessing

Ancient of Days, whose spirit brooded upon the face of the deep in the dawn of creation, we lift up our hearts in thanksgiving for the graciousness of the earth our home. We walk with joy under the life-giving sun, the center star of our long voyage in the heavens. We welcome the nourishing waters upon the face of the planet, with all its trees and flowers. We cherish the solemn flow of great rivers, the mysteries of our mountains, the everlasting sea. We look with joy into the eyes of love and hear with gladness the voices that draw us home to friends and families.

For all the wisdom of our forebears in every land we offer thanks. For the courage to find new ways of life in the midst of ancient blessing and blight, we offer thanks. We pray a special blessing upon the young who are moving into their unknown future, that they may remember their fathers and mothers with joy and be free to build the new life that they alone can dream and fulfill. Bind us all, young and old, in one communion of freedom and charity, that together we may trust life and live unafraid.

Bless thou our coming in and our going forth this day and forevermore. *Amen.*

Prayer for Hope

O Thou who art the music of the world, the hidden song within all singing, and the light of all lights, grant us such fullness in our lives with thy grace that we may offer heartfelt praise and labor toward a more just society, a more loving humanity, and a more beautiful earth.

In the world's night we are bereft of power and hope unless some uncontrived shining visit us, some radiance we had not dared to trust. Let us not fear to know in the world's night that we are incomplete, that we have done more than is right and less than is required of us, that our days are numbered, that we must lose all we have and all we remember, that we must die.

Shine forth out of the world's night in love's large liberty, that we may rise from our falling and stand firm in joy and good hope. Defend our days against chaos and despair by such concord of grace that our deeds will serve as an offering of thanksgiving.

We offer this prayer for those we love, for our children's future, for the children of all people, for the sake of the human family in its most precious, dangerous, and courageous journey through time. *Amen.*

Prayer of Thanksgiving

O thou who hast tuned our hearts to praise, thou source of our singing and perfect receiver of our offering of song, we rejoice in thy house with thanksgiving. Before ever the world was made and darkness was upon the face of the deep, there was Love and Wisdom's Word. And then there came light, and the stars and planets, the waters, the earth, and all the multitude of green plants and boughs, and the creatures of sea and land and air, and at last thy children, the peoples of the earth. And over all and in all, an undying music, an everlasting harmony to bear and resolve all dissonance, to sound forth in strength and gentleness, to bring tidings of order and of freedom.

All thy creatures offer praise with rejoicing, each in its own voice; all thy creatures suffer hurt and make plaintive music of their misery; all thy creatures are renewed in thy springtime cadences. We ask for no single tone of life: We know that tone and time must ever change, sometimes bitter, sometimes serene. But we pray that the singing itself may never end, that songs of innocence and songs of experience, bright songs and sad songs, may rise from the fountains of our lives unendingly. In the first cries of infancy, in the songs of childhood, in the music of our strength, and in the voices of our oldest age we offer our thanksgiving, our prayers, and our benedictions unto thee, the Master Singer, the Eternal Music. *Amen.*

Prayer for Humankind

O Thou who hast created the worlds and hast given the benediction of thy spirit among thy human creatures, how can we say our thanks and how shall we give voice to the fullness of our gratitude? For all gifts are most dear and precious among us. Though they must vanish as flowers and though we too must reach an end of days, we give the heart's deepest thanks.

Let thy justice penetrate to us all as we hunger and thirst for righteousness. Strengthen the weak hands and the feeble knees, that each life shall not pass without an offering and a glory.

In this house of joy we remember all distant and cherished persons whom we hold in affection and esteem. We remember the living and the dead in whose lives we have found light and love. We join ourselves—by deed and dedication, in song and wisdom—to our humankind, to its glory, its struggle and agony, and its foundation in everlasting holiness. *Amen.*

Prayer of Celebration

O thou whose power brooded over the multitude of life upon the face of the earth, we offer before thee this day the heart of thanksgiving praise. All thy creatures praise thee in the dances of their living. The rhythms of sea waves and land swell, of wind and stillness, the green and the barren, the day and the night, death and life, all cry out the song of the ancient prophet:

Holy, Holy, Holy is the Lord of Hosts
The whole earth is full of thy glory!

The ancestors, though dead, yet add their songs to the endless music. The children yet to come are as voices dreaming toward song. In the brightness of our own moment of life, the singing goes on. If we close our eyes, the light still shines. If we shut our ears, the voice still cries within. We pray that thy music may penetrate to all sorrowing hearts, that their grief and pain may not cut them off from the holiness of life.

In the presence of thy sacred mystery, we say *Amen*.

Prayer for Spring

O thou who art the strength of hills and earth and the love and goodness in the soul of humanity, at this season of glory and light and growing green, we give thee the heart's deepest thanks for all thy bounty.

Thine is the strength that has carried our people through their winter pilgrimages; thou hast shared the pains of our ordeals and hast known our deaths and despairings. And in the mystery of rebirth, thou hast seen thy children live to rejoice and create and hast launched them into new worlds of life and love.

We cannot comprehend these mysteries. We cannot force their might or rule their power. We can only bow before thee in humility and profound thanksgiving. With praise and adoration and all fullness of heart, we render to thee the glory forever.
Amen.

Prayer of Remembrance

Unto thee, O Lord, our Creator and Sustainer, we offer
our thanksgiving as we recall in thy house the visitations of
thy holiness.

We remember with joy the many tiny children who have been
brought to the font of living waters and have been named and
dedicated to the goodness of life by our pledges and our prayers.
We remember the happy troops of children and youth who—by
song, dance, drama, and speech—have brought their newfound
powers and graces as an offering to thee. We remember with
delight all those cherished persons who in thy sanctuary have
taken each other in holy matrimony and have made their
married state honorable by their faithful keeping of it. We recall
with thankful hearts those who have been ordained to thy
ministry, who have carried our trust, our blessing, and our
prayers into the service of the church. We remember all skillful
artists who have shown forth thy spirit in motions of the dance
and of melody, in storied images of grief and of ecstasy, in new
visions of order. We are grateful for the power of the spoken
word in our common worship, for the transforming of stones
into a house where goods are praised and evils faced, where
sorrows are healed and high purposes kindled.

In silence and in deepest thanksgiving, O Lord, we call to mind
those many beloved ones, whose lives we have cherished and
whom we have honored in the time of their death. Their earthly

remains are laid to rest amid the foundations of thy house; their spirits speak to us in our lifted vaults and shining windows.

As we go forth to our several ways and callings, may we remain united in fellowship and charity by the holy communion of this hour, each of us making our offering to the world of the living and saying in our hearts, "Lord, I have loved the habitation of thy house and the place where thine honor dwelleth." *Amen.*

Notes

Art and the Religious Life was presented to the Religious Arts Guild of the American Unitarian Association in Boston, Massachusetts, May 1964.

Imaginative Truth and the Creator was delivered as a sermon at the All Souls Unitarian Church in Tulsa, Oklahoma, February 1964.

The Modest Doorway of Craft was delivered as a sermon to the Unitarian Universalist Fellowship in Decatur, Illinois, September 1988.

Music and Wild Horses was delivered as a sermon at the First Unitarian Church of St. Louis, Missouri, September 1969.

Superstition, Doubt and Faith was delivered as a sermon at the First Unitarian Society of Madison, Wisconsin, November 1983.

Living Religion and a Liberal Tradition was published as Chapter 10 of *Existentialism and Religious Liberalism* (Boston: Beacon Press, 1962), 105–115. Reprinted and adapted with permission.

Myth and the Modern World was published as "The Uses of Myth in an Age of Science," in *Zygon: Journal of Religion and Science* 3, no. 2 (June 1968): 205–219. Reprinted and adapted with permission.

A New Story of Creation was delivered as a sermon at the First Unitarian Church of St. Louis, Missouri, November 2000.

The Greek Hero and the Biblical Anti-hero was presented at the Ecumenical Institute for Advanced Theological Studies in Jerusalem, Israel, February 1976.

Judaic Mythology in Modern Christianity was delivered as a sermon at the Carbondale Unitarian Fellowship in Carbondale, Illinois, Easter 1978.

The Incredible Folklore of Easter was delivered as a sermon at the Carbondale Unitarian Fellowship in Carbondale, Illinois, March 1991.

Hope and the Holy Spirit was delivered as "Giving Life: A Commentary on the Concept of the Holy Spirit" at the Unitarian Universalist Church in Silver Spring, Maryland, June 1980.

Divine Justice in the Hebrew Bible was delivered as a sermon at the Carbondale Unitarian Fellowship in Carbondale, Illinois, March 1997.

Through the Rose Window is an amalgam of two sermons given at the First Unitarian Church of Chicago, the first in November 1962, and the second in September 1996.